# WORLD LEADERS

## People Who Shaped the World

# WORLD LEADERS

**People Who Shaped the World**

Europe

Rob Nagel • Anne Commire

AN IMPRINT OF
GALE RESEARCH INC.

# World Leaders:
*People Who Shaped the World*

Rob Nagel and Anne Commire

## Staff

Sonia Benson, U·X·L *Associate Developmental Editor*
Kathleen L. Witman, U·X·L *Assistant Developmental Editor*
Thomas L. Romig, U·X·L *Publisher*

Mary Kelley, *Production Associate*
Evi Seoud, *Assistant Production Manager*
Mary Beth Trimper, *Production Director*

Pamela A. E. Galbreath, *Cover and Page Designer*
Cynthia Baldwin, *Art Director*

Keith Reed, *Permissions Associate (Pictures)*
Margaret A. Chamberlain, *Permissions Supervisor (Pictures)*

The Graphix Group, *Typesetting*

Library of Congress Cataloging-in-Publication Data
World leaders: people who shaped the world / {edited by} Rob Nagel,
   Anne Commire.
     p.  cm.
   Includes biographical references and index.
   ISBN 0-8103-9768-4 (set)
   1. Kings and rulers --Biography. 2. Heads of state--Biography. 3. Revolutionaries--
   Biography. 4. Statesmen--Biography. I. Nagel, Rob. II. Commire, Anne.
D107.W65 1994
   920.02--dc20
                                                94-20544
                                                      CIP
                                                       AC

This book is printed on acid-free paper that meets the minimum requirements of American National Standard for Information Sciences—Permanence Paper for Printed Library Materials, ANSI Z39.48-1984.

ISBN 0-8103-9768-4 (Set)

ISBN 0-8103-9769-2 (Volume 1)
ISBN 0-8103-9770-6 (Volume 2)
ISBN 0-8103-9771-4 (Volume 3)

Printed in the United States of America

Published simultaneously in the United Kingdom by Gale Research International Limited (An affiliated company of Gale Research Inc.)

# Contents

## VOLUME 2: EUROPE

## VOLUME 3: NORTH AND SOUTH AMERICA

# Preface

Through 120 biographical sketches in three volumes, *World Leaders: People Who Shaped the World* presents a diverse range of historical figures. Many of those profiled are political or military leaders whose achievements have been evident and far-reaching. Others featured may not be as conspicuous to the beginning student of history, but their achievements—considering the social context of the eras in which they lived and the barriers against which they fought—are no less great.

The individuals chosen for inclusion in *World Leaders* fall into one or more of the following categories:

- Those who significantly changed their nation or empire, affecting its—or the world's—course permanently or for a very long time.
- Those who exhibited great qualities in many areas—military, politics, art, religion, philosophy.
- Those who struggled against the forced limitations of gender, race, or social standing to achieve their ideals, leaving a trail for others to follow.

• Those who offered the world new ideas, options, or directions.

Each volume of *World Leaders* begins with a listing of the leaders by country and a timeline showing the chronological relationship among the profiled leaders, the incidents marking their lives, and certain other historical events.

Many sketches in *World Leaders* begin with a short discussion of the social or political environment in which these individuals arose. Where possible, childhood and educational experiences of the chosen leaders have been highlighted. Philosophical or religious ideas or movements that directed the course of the leaders' actions are explained in the text. Some of these ideas or movements, such as Stoicism or the Enlightenment, are given a fuller discussion in sidebars, more than a dozen of which are sprinkled throughout the three volumes. Other sidebars present varied topics—from the U.S. cost in the Vietnam War to a Shaker hymn—that are both informative and interesting.

Each biographical sketch in *World Leaders* contains a portrait of the profiled leader and the date and the place of that person's birth and death, or the dates of his or her reign. To provide readers with a clearer understanding of the geographical descriptions in the text, maps are placed within some sketches. A comprehensive subject index concludes each volume.

## Acknowledgments

We wish to extend a humble note of thanks to the U·X·L family: Tom Romig, for graciously handing us this project; Kathleen Witman, for insightfully emending the style of the text; and, finally, Sonia Benson, for gently shepherding the work to its completion.

We welcome any comments on this work and suggestions for future volumes of *World Leaders*. Please write: Editors, *World Leaders,* U·X·L, Gale Research Inc., 835 Penobscot Bldg., Detroit, Michigan 48226-4094; call toll-free: 1-800-877-4253; or fax: 313-961-6348.

# World Leaders by Country

*A listing of leaders by the central country or countries in which they ruled or made changes. When possible, ancient empires, city-states, and kingdoms have been listed with an asterisk under the modern-day country in which they were once located.*

**Argentina:**

José de San Martín
  (1778-1850)
Eva Marie Duarte de Perón
  (1919-1952)
Juan Domingo Perón
  (1895-1974)

**Assyria** (ancient empire including vast region of western Asia):
Ashurbanipal
  (c. 700-c. 626 B.C.)

**Babylon** (ancient city-state near present day Baghdad, Iraq):

Hammurabi
  (ruled c. 1792-1759 B.C.)

**Bolivia:**

Simón Bolívar
  (1783-1830)

**Canada:**

Samuel de Champlain
  (c. 1570-1635)

**Carthage** (city-state in present-day Tunisia):
Hannibal
  (247-183 B.C.)

## China:

Chiang Kai-shek
  (1887-1975)
Confucius
  (c. 551-c. 479 B.C.)
Lao-tzu
  (c. sixth century B.C.)
Mao Zedong
  (1893-1976)
Qin Shi Huang-di
  (259-210 B.C.)
Zhao Kuang-yin
  (927-976)

## Colombia:

Simón Bolívar
  (1783-1830)

## Cuba:

Ernesto "Ché" Guevara
  (1928-1967)
José Martí
  (1853-1895)

## Denmark:

Canute I, the Great
  (c. 995-1035)
Margaret I
  (1353-1412)

## Egypt:

Cleopatra VII
  (69-30 B.C.)
Hatshepsut
  (c. 1520-c. 1468 B.C.)
Moses
  (c. late 13th century–
  c. early 11th century B.C.)

Gamal Abdal Nasser
  (1918-1970)
Ptolemy I Soter
  (367-285 B.C.)
Ramses II
  (c. 1315-c. 1225 B.C.)

## England:

Alfred the Great
  (848-c. 900)
Canute I, the Great
  (c. 995-1035)
Winston Churchill
  (1874-1965)
Elizabeth I
  (1533-1603)
Victoria
  (1819-1901)
William the Conqueror
  (c. 1027-1087)

## Ethiopia:

Haile Selassie I
  (1892-1975)

## France:

Eleanor of Aquitaine
  (1122-1204)
Joan of Arc
  (c. 1412-1431)
Louis XIV
  (1638-1715)
Napoleon I Bonaparte
  (1769-1821)

## Germany:

Adolf Hitler
  (1889-1945)

Martin Luther
   (1483-1546)
Rudolf I, of Habsburg
   (1218-1291)

## Haiti:

Toussaint L'Ouverture
   (1743-1803)

## Hungary:

Stephen I
   (c. 973-1038)

## India:

Akbar
   (1542-1605)
Mohandas Gandhi
   (1869-1948)
Jawaharlal Nehru
   (1889-1964)
Siddhartha
   (c. 563-c. 483 B.C.)
Mother Teresa
   (1910—)

## Iran (formerly Persia):

Abbas I
   (1571-1629)
Cyrus II, the Great
   (c. 590-c. 529)
Ruhollah Khomeini
   (c. 1902-1989)
Zoroaster
   (c. 588-c. 511 B.C.)

## Ireland:

Saint Patrick
   (c. 395-c. 460)

## Israel:

David Ben-Gurion
   (1886-1973)
King David
   (ruled 1010-970 B.C.)
Jesus of Nazareth
   (c. 6 B.C.-c. A.D. 26)
Moses
   (c. late 13th century–
   c. early 11th century B.C.)

## Italy (also see Roman Empire):

Francis of Assisi
   (1182-1226)
John XXIII
   (1881-1963)

## Japan:

Fujiwara Michinaga
   (966-1028)

## Kenya:

Jomo Kenyatta
   (1891-1978)

## Macedonia:

Alexander the Great
   (356-323 B.C.)

## Mexico:

Juana Inés de la Cruz
   (1648-1695)
Emiliano Zapata
   (1879-1919)
*Tenochtitlán:*

Moctezuma II
  (c. 1480-1520)


**Mongolia:**

Genghis Khan
  (c. 1162-1227)


**Norway:**

Canute I, the Great
  (c. 995-1035)
Margaret I
  (1353-1412)


**North Vietnam:**

Ho Chi Minh
  (1890-1969)


**Pannonia**] (area in present-
  day Hungary and eastern
  Austria):
Attila the Hun
  (c. 370-453)


**Prussia** (former state of
  Central Europe, including
  parts of present-day
  Germany and Poland):
Frederick II, the Great
  (1712-1786)
Karl Marx
  (1818-1883)


**Roman Empire:**

Augustus
  (63 B.C.-A.D. 14)
Julius Caesar

(100-44 B.C.)
Charlemagne
  (c. 742-814)
Charles V
  (1500-1558)
Constantine I
  (285-337)
Frederick I (Barbarossa)
  (1123-1190)
Gregory I, the Great
  (c. 540-604)
Marcus Aurelius
  (121-180)
Otto I, the Great
  (912-973)
Rudolf I, of Habsburg
  (1218-1291)


**Russia:**

Catherine II, the Great
  (1729-1796)
Gorbachev, Mikhail
  (1931—)
Ivan IV, the Terrible
  (1530-1584)
Vladimir Lenin
  (1870-1924)
Alexander Nevsky
  (c. 1220-1263)


**Saudi Arabia:**

Muhammad (c. 570-632)


**Scotland:**

Mary, Queen of Scots
  (1542-1587)
Robert I, the Bruce
  (1274-1329)

## Senegal:

Léopold Sédar Senghor
  (1906—)

## Spain:

Ferdinand II
  (1452-1516)
Isabella I
  (1451-1504)

## Sweden:

Gustavus Adolphus
  (1594-1632)
Margaret I
  (1353-1412)

## Syria:

*Palmyra:*
Zenobia
  (ruled 267-272)

## Turkey:

*Byzantine Empire:*
Irene of Athens
  (c. 752-803)
Theodora
  (c. 500-548)
*Ottoman Empire:*
Osman I
  (1259-1326)
Suleiman
  (c. 1494-1566)

## United Republic of Tanzania:

Julius K. Nyerere
  (1922—)

## United States:

Jane Addams
  (1860-1935)
Susan B. Anthony
  (1820-1906)
William Bradford
  (1590-1657)
Chief Joseph
  (1840-1905)
Crazy Horse
  (1841-1877)
Frederick Douglass
  (1818-1895)
W. E. B. Du Bois
  (1868-1963)
Benjamin Franklin
  (1706-1790)
Ulysses S. Grant
  (1822-1885)
Thomas Jefferson
  (1743-1826)
John F. Kennedy
  (1917-1963)
Martin Luther King, Jr.
  (1929-1968)
Mother Ann Lee
  (1736-1784)
Robert E. Lee
  (1807-1870)
Abraham Lincoln
  (1809-1865)
Malcolm X
  (1925-1965)
Thurgood Marshall
  (1908-1993)
Increase Mather
  (1639-1723)
Thomas Paine
  (1737-1809)

Eleanor Roosevelt
   (1884-1962)
Franklin Roosevelt
   (1882-1945)
Sitting Bull
   (c. 1830-1890)
John Smith
   (c. 1580-1631)
Elizabeth Cady Stanton
   (1815-1902)
Tecumseh
   (c. 1768-1813)
Sojourner Truth
   (c. 1797-1883)
Harriet Tubman
   (c. 1820-1913)
Booker T. Washington
   (1856-1915)
George Washington
   (1732-1799)
Roger Williams
   (c. 1603-1683)

## Venezuela:

Simón Bolívar
   (1783-1830)

# WORLD LEADERS

## People Who Shaped the World

*Egyptian Pyramids*

# Timeline

**3000 B.C.** —————— **1500 B.C.** —————————————— **550 B.C.**

**1010-970 B.C.**

**1: David** unites
Israel and Judah
in a kingdom
centered at
Jerusalem

**c. 1792-1750 B.C.**

**1: Hammurabi** creates empire of Babylonia
and devises his famous law code

---

**c. 2680–1200 B.C. • Ancient Egypt**

**c. 2680-2526 B.C. • 1:** Building of the Great Pyramids near Giza,
Egypt

**c. 1490-1470 B.C. • 1: Hatshepsut** proclaims herself "king" of
Egypt and rules as pharaoh

**c. 1250 B.C. • 1: Ramses II** builds colossal temple at Abu Simbel

**c. 1200 B.C. • 1: Moses** leads the Hebrews out of slavery in Egypt
to the land of Canaan

---

**c. 670-626 B.C.**

**1: Ashurbanipal**
creates a great
library in
Nineveh, the
capital city of the
Assyrian Empire

---

**c. 6th century B.C. • Philosophy and Religion**

**c. 6th century B.C. • 1: Lao-tzu** reportedly writes his moral
philosophy in the *Tao Te Ching*

**c. 550-511 B.C. • 1: Zoroaster** spreads his new religion
throughout the Persian Empire

**c. 528 B.C. • 1: Siddhartha** founds new religion of Buddhism in
India

**c. 520 B.C. • 1: Confucius** begins teaching a new moral
philosophy in China

---

**c. 550 B.C.**

**1: Cyrus II, the Great**
conquers Media and begins
building the Persian Empire

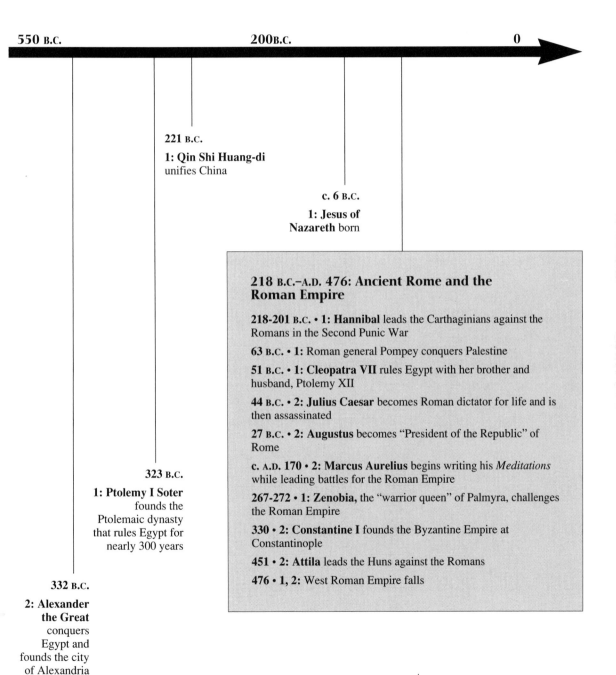

1 = Volume 1: Asia and Africa
2 = Volume 2: Europe
3 = Volume 3: North and South America

550 B.C.                    200B.C.                    0 →

221 B.C.

1: Qin Shi Huang-di
unifies China

c. 6 B.C.

1: Jesus of
Nazareth born

218 B.C.–A.D. 476: Ancient Rome and the
Roman Empire

218-201 B.C. • 1: Hannibal leads the Carthaginians against the
Romans in the Second Punic War

63 B.C. • 1: Roman general Pompey conquers Palestine

51 B.C. • 1: Cleopatra VII rules Egypt with her brother and
husband, Ptolemy XII

44 B.C. • 2: Julius Caesar becomes Roman dictator for life and is
then assassinated

27 B.C. • 2: Augustus becomes "President of the Republic" of
Rome

c. A.D. 170 • 2: Marcus Aurelius begins writing his *Meditations*
while leading battles for the Roman Empire

267-272 • 1: Zenobia, the "warrior queen" of Palmyra, challenges
the Roman Empire

330 • 2: Constantine I founds the Byzantine Empire at
Constantinople

451 • 2: Attila leads the Huns against the Romans

476 • 1, 2: West Roman Empire falls

323 B.C.

1: Ptolemy I Soter
founds the
Ptolemaic dynasty
that rules Egypt for
nearly 300 years

332 B.C.

2: Alexander
the Great
conquers
Egypt and
founds the city
of Alexandria

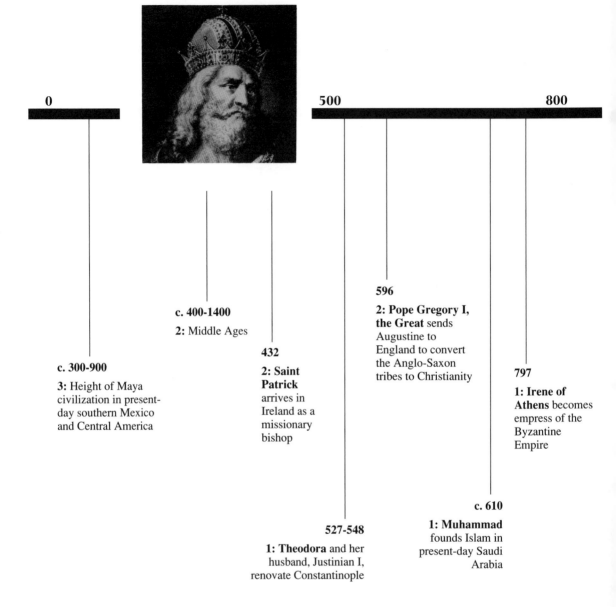

*Charlemagne*

**0**

**500**

**800**

**c. 400-1400**
**2:** Middle Ages

**432**
**2: Saint Patrick** arrives in Ireland as a missionary bishop

**596**
**2: Pope Gregory I, the Great** sends Augustine to England to convert the Anglo-Saxon tribes to Christianity

**c. 300-900**
**3:** Height of Maya civilization in present-day southern Mexico and Central America

**797**
**1: Irene of Athens** becomes empress of the Byzantine Empire

**c. 610**
**1: Muhammad** founds Islam in present-day Saudi Arabia

**527-548**
**1: Theodora** and her husband, Justinian I, renovate Constantinople

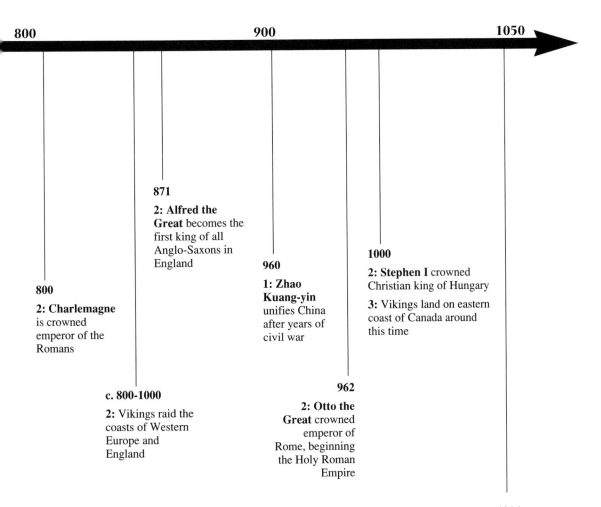

1 = Volume 1: Asia and Africa
2 = Volume 2: Europe
3 = Volume 3: North and South America

800　　　　　　　　　　　　900　　　　　　　　　　　1050

**871**

**2: Alfred the Great** becomes the first king of all Anglo-Saxons in England

**800**

**2: Charlemagne** is crowned emperor of the Romans

**960**

**1: Zhao Kuang-yin** unifies China after years of civil war

**1000**

**2: Stephen I** crowned Christian king of Hungary

**3:** Vikings land on eastern coast of Canada around this time

**c. 800-1000**

**2:** Vikings raid the coasts of Western Europe and England

**962**

**2: Otto the Great** crowned emperor of Rome, beginning the Holy Roman Empire

**1016**

**1: Fujiwara Michinaga** assumes behind-the-scenes political power in Japan

**2:** Viking **Canute I, the Great** begins rule as king of England, Denmark, and Norway

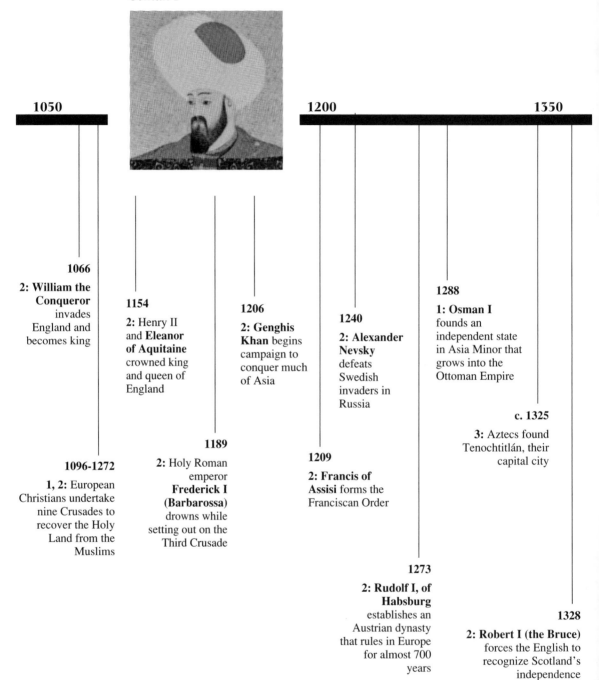

*Osman I*

**1050**

**1200**

**1350**

**1066**

**2: William the Conqueror** invades England and becomes king

**1154**

**2: Henry II** and **Eleanor of Aquitaine** crowned king and queen of England

**1206**

**2: Genghis Khan** begins campaign to conquer much of Asia

**1240**

**2: Alexander Nevsky** defeats Swedish invaders in Russia

**1288**

**1: Osman I** founds an independent state in Asia Minor that grows into the Ottoman Empire

**c. 1325**

**3:** Aztecs found Tenochtitlán, their capital city

**1096-1272**

**1, 2:** European Christians undertake nine Crusades to recover the Holy Land from the Muslims

**1189**

**2:** Holy Roman emperor **Frederick I (Barbarossa)** drowns while setting out on the Third Crusade

**1209**

**2: Francis of Assisi** forms the Franciscan Order

**1273**

**2: Rudolf I, of Habsburg** establishes an Austrian dynasty that rules in Europe for almost 700 years

**1328**

**2: Robert I (the Bruce)** forces the English to recognize Scotland's independence

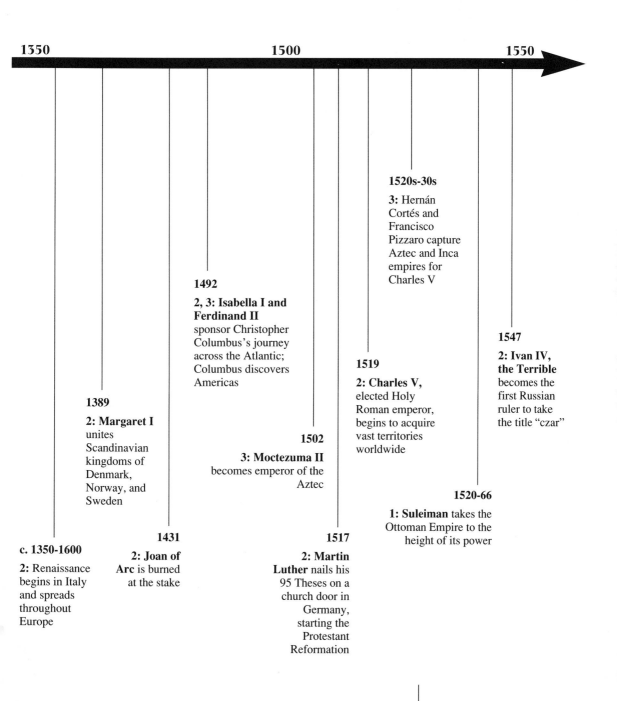

1 = Volume 1: Asia and Africa
2 = Volume 2: Europe
3 = Volume 3: North and South America

1350                    1500                  1550

**1520s-30s**

**3:** Hernán Cortés and Francisco Pizarro capture Aztec and Inca empires for Charles V

**1492**

**2, 3: Isabella I and Ferdinand II** sponsor Christopher Columbus's journey across the Atlantic; Columbus discovers Americas

**1547**

**2: Ivan IV, the Terrible** becomes the first Russian ruler to take the title "czar"

**1389**

**2: Margaret I** unites Scandinavian kingdoms of Denmark, Norway, and Sweden

**1519**

**2: Charles V,** elected Holy Roman emperor, begins to acquire vast territories worldwide

**1502**

**3: Moctezuma II** becomes emperor of the Aztec

**c. 1350-1600**

**2:** Renaissance begins in Italy and spreads throughout Europe

**1431**

**2: Joan of Arc** is burned at the stake

**1517**

**2: Martin Luther** nails his 95 Theses on a church door in Germany, starting the Protestant Reformation

**1520-66**

**1: Suleiman** takes the Ottoman Empire to the height of its power

*Elizabeth I*

**1550**

**1600**

**1700**

**1588**

**2: Elizabeth I**'s navy defeats the Spanish Armada

**1611-30**

**2: Gustavus Adolphus** forms a Swedish empire

**1688**

**3: Increase Mather** secures charter for the Massachusetts Bay Colony

**1587**

**1: Abbas I** begins rule as shah of Persia (Iran)

**2: Mary, Queen of Scots** is beheaded by the order of the English queen **Elizabeth I**

**1654**

**2: Louis XIV** is crowned king of France

**1556**

**1: Akbar** assumes throne of the Mughal Empire in India

**1607–1636 • Settlements in North America**

**1607 • 3: John Smith** and others found Jamestown

**1608 • 3: Samuel de Champlain** founds Quebec

**1620 • 3: William Bradford** and other Puritans found Plymouth

**1636 • 3: Roger Williams** founds Providence, Rhode Island

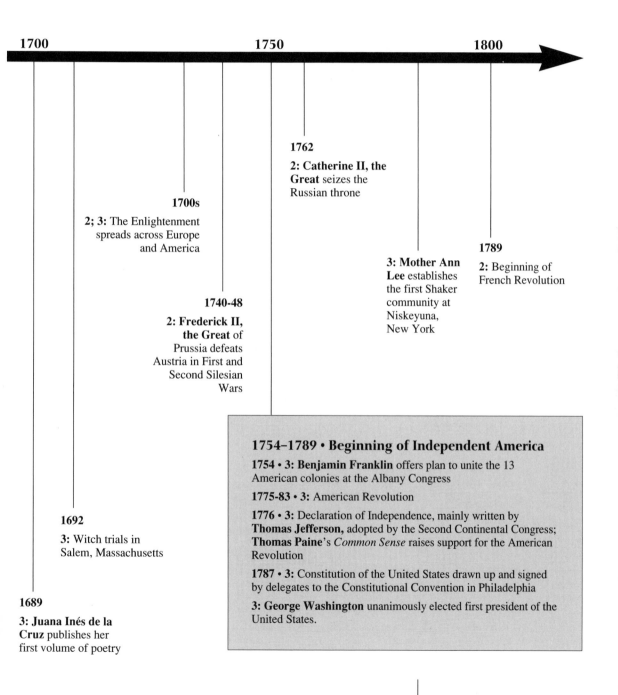

1 = Volume 1: Asia and Africa
2 = Volume 2: Europe
3 = Volume 3: North and South America

1700                              1750                      1800

**1762**

**2: Catherine II, the Great** seizes the Russian throne

**1700s**

**2; 3:** The Enlightenment spreads across Europe and America

**1789**

**2:** Beginning of French Revolution

**3: Mother Ann Lee** establishes the first Shaker community at Niskeyuna, New York

**1740-48**

**2: Frederick II, the Great** of Prussia defeats Austria in First and Second Silesian Wars

**1692**

**3:** Witch trials in Salem, Massachusetts

**1689**

**3: Juana Inés de la Cruz** publishes her first volume of poetry

**1754–1789 • Beginning of Independent America**

**1754 • 3: Benjamin Franklin** offers plan to unite the 13 American colonies at the Albany Congress

**1775-83 • 3:** American Revolution

**1776 • 3:** Declaration of Independence, mainly written by **Thomas Jefferson,** adopted by the Second Continental Congress; **Thomas Paine**'s *Common Sense* raises support for the American Revolution

**1787 • 3:** Constitution of the United States drawn up and signed by delegates to the Constitutional Convention in Philadelphia

**3: George Washington** unanimously elected first president of the United States.

## Simón Bolívar

**1800**

**1820**

**1850**

**1817**
**3: José de San Martín** battles Spanish forces in Chile

**1837-1901**
**2:** Reign of England's Queen Victoria II

**1812**
**3: Tecumseh** and English forces capture Detroit

**1819**
**3: Simón Bolívar** proclaimed president of Greater Colombia

**1848**
**3: Karl Marx** and Friedrich Engels publish the *Communist Manifesto*

**1804**
**2: Napoleon I Bonaparte** is crowned emperor of France

**1812-15**
**2, 3:** War of 1812 between the U.S. and England

**1801**
**3: Toussaint L'Ouverture** conquers Spanish colony of Santo Domingo

### 1831–1870 • Slavery and the American Civil War

**1831 • 3:** Nat Turner leads a bloody slave uprising in Virginia

**1841 • 3: Frederick Douglass** gives his first abolitionist speech

**1850 • 3: Harriet Tubman** leads her first party of slaves to freedom on the Underground Railroad; **Sojourner Truth** publishes her autobiography, *Narrative of Sojourner Truth*

**1859 • 3:** Abolitionist John Brown is hanged after seizing the government arsenal at Harpers Ferry, Virginia

**1861-65 • 3:** American Civil War

**1862 • 3: Robert E. Lee** defeats the Union forces at the Seven Days' battle and the second battle of Bull Run

**1863 • 3: Abraham Lincoln** issues the Emancipation Proclamation; **Ulysses S. Grant** defeats the Confederate forces at Vicksburg

**1865 • 3: Lee** surrenders to Grant at Appomattox Courthouse; **Lincoln** assassinated by John Wilkes Booth at Ford's Theater

**1868 • 3:** U.S. Congress adopts the Fourteenth Amendment, recognizing former slaves as U.S. citizens

**1870 • 3:** Fifteenth Amendment of U.S. Constitution extends voting rights to all black males

**Timeline**

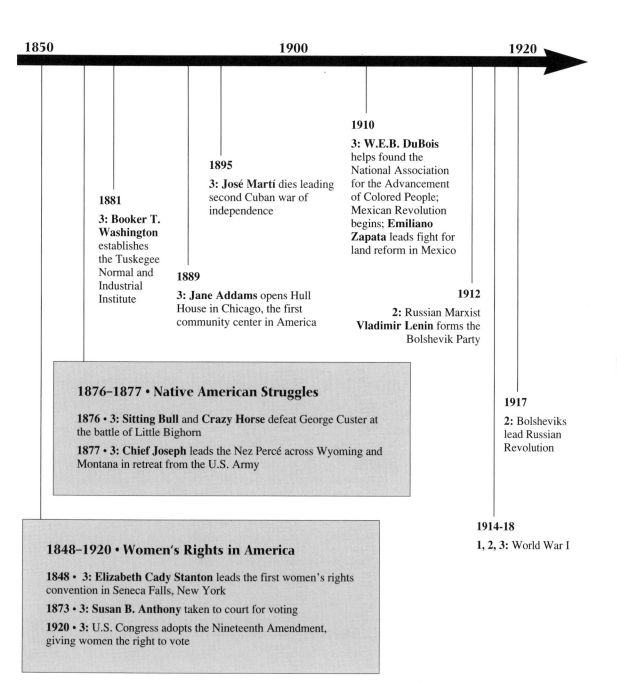

1 = **Volume 1: Asia and Africa**
2 = **Volume 2: Europe**
3 = **Volume 3: North and South America**

1850                    1900                    1920

**1910**

**3: W.E.B. DuBois**
helps found the
National Association
for the Advancement
of Colored People;
Mexican Revolution
begins; **Emiliano
Zapata** leads fight for
land reform in Mexico

**1895**

**3: José Martí** dies leading
second Cuban war of
independence

**1881**

**3: Booker T.
Washington**
establishes
the Tuskegee
Normal and
Industrial
Institute

**1889**

**3: Jane Addams** opens Hull
House in Chicago, the first
community center in America

**1912**

2: Russian Marxist
**Vladimir Lenin** forms the
Bolshevik Party

**1876–1877 • Native American Struggles**

**1876 • 3: Sitting Bull** and **Crazy Horse** defeat George Custer at
the battle of Little Bighorn

**1877 • 3: Chief Joseph** leads the Nez Percé across Wyoming and
Montana in retreat from the U.S. Army

**1917**

2: Bolsheviks
lead Russian
Revolution

**1848–1920 • Women's Rights in America**

**1848 • 3: Elizabeth Cady Stanton** leads the first women's rights
convention in Seneca Falls, New York

**1873 • 3: Susan B. Anthony** taken to court for voting

**1920 • 3:** U.S. Congress adopts the Nineteenth Amendment,
giving women the right to vote

**1914-18**

**1, 2, 3:** World War I

*Adolf Hitler*

**1920**

**1935**

**1946**

**1940**

**2: Winston Churchill** is named prime minister of England

**1926**

**1: Chiang Kai-shek** leads his Nationalist army in the Northern Expedition to unify China

**1933**

**2: Adolf Hitler** is named chancellor of Germany

**3: Franklin D. Roosevelt** begins his New Deal program

**1939-45**

**1, 2, 3:** World War II

**1946**

**3: Eleanor Roosevelt** appointed chairperson of the United Nations Commission on Human Rights

**1929**

**3:** Stock-market crash in the U.S. marks the beginning of the Great Depression

**1935**

**1: Haile Selassie I** leads his Ethiopian army against the invading Italian forces of Benito Mussolini

**1946**

**3: Juan Domingo Perón** elected president of Argentina

**1919–1947 • Indian Independence**

**1919 • 1: Mohandas Gandhi** organizes his first nationwide nonviolent demonstration protesting English rule in India

**1947 • 1: Jawaharlal Nehru** becomes the first prime minister of an independent India

1 = **Volume 1: Asia and Africa**
2 = **Volume 2: Europe**
3 = **Volume 3: North and South America**

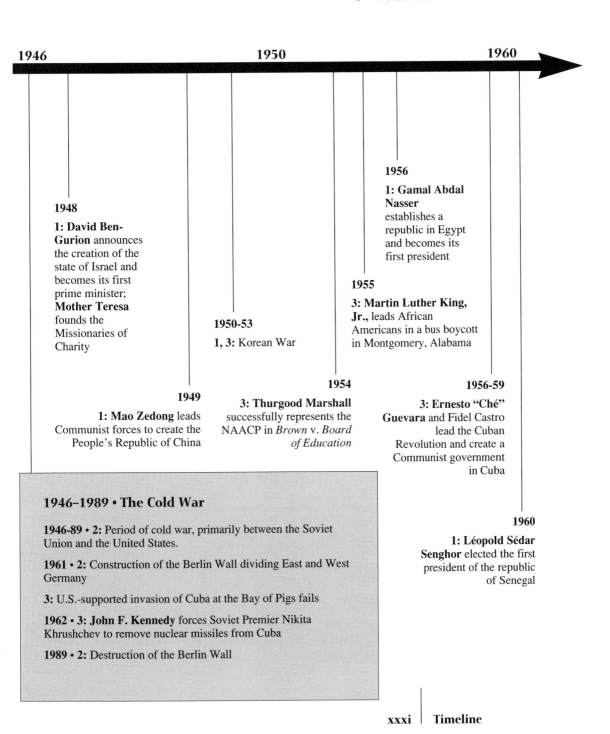

**1946**                **1950**               **1960**

**1956**

**1: Gamal Abdal Nasser** establishes a republic in Egypt and becomes its first president

**1948**

**1: David Ben-Gurion** announces the creation of the state of Israel and becomes its first prime minister; **Mother Teresa** founds the Missionaries of Charity

**1955**

**3: Martin Luther King, Jr.,** leads African Americans in a bus boycott in Montgomery, Alabama

**1950-53**

**1, 3:** Korean War

**1954**

**3: Thurgood Marshall** successfully represents the NAACP in *Brown* v. *Board of Education*

**1949**

**1: Mao Zedong** leads Communist forces to create the People's Republic of China

**1956-59**

**3: Ernesto "Ché" Guevara** and Fidel Castro lead the Cuban Revolution and create a Communist government in Cuba

**1960**

**1: Léopold Sédar Senghor** elected the first president of the republic of Senegal

**1946–1989 • The Cold War**

**1946-89 • 2:** Period of cold war, primarily between the Soviet Union and the United States.

**1961 • 2:** Construction of the Berlin Wall dividing East and West Germany

**3:** U.S.-supported invasion of Cuba at the Bay of Pigs fails

**1962 • 3: John F. Kennedy** forces Soviet Premier Nikita Khrushchev to remove nuclear missiles from Cuba

**1989 • 2:** Destruction of the Berlin Wall

*John F. Kennedy*

**1960**

**1965**

**1980**

**1962**

**2: Pope John XXI** opens the Second Vatican Council in Rome

**1964**

**1: Jomo Kenyatta** becomes the first president of the newly independent Kenya; **Julius K. Nyerere** unites Tanganyika and Zanzibar to form Tanzania, and becomes its first president

**1969**

**3:** U.S. astronaut Neil Armstrong becomes the first person to walk on the moon

**1979**

**1: Ruhollah Khomeini** creates an Islamic state in Iran

## 1963–1968 • Assassinations in America

**1963 • 3: John F. Kennedy** assassinated in Dallas, Texas

**1965 • 3: Malcolm X** assassinated in New York

**1968 • 3: Martin Luther King, Jr.,** assassinated in Memphis, Tennessee

## 1954–1975 • Conflict in Vietnam

**1954 • 1: Ho Chi Minh** becomes president of Communist North Vietnam after Vietnamese forces defeat the French

**1961-73 • 3:** U.S. takes part in the Vietnam War

**1975 • 1:** North Vietnam defeats South Vietnam, uniting the country under a Communist government

1 = **Volume 1: Asia and Africa**
2 = **Volume 2: Europe**
3 = **Volume 3: North and South America**

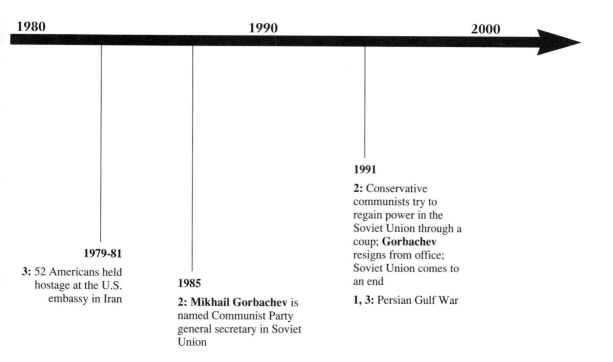

| 1980 | 1990 | 2000 |

**1991**

**2:** Conservative communists try to regain power in the Soviet Union through a coup; **Gorbachev** resigns from office; Soviet Union comes to an end

**1, 3:** Persian Gulf War

**1979-81**

**3:** 52 Americans held hostage at the U.S. embassy in Iran

**1985**

**2: Mikhail Gorbachev** is named Communist Party general secretary in Soviet Union

*Mikhail Gorbachev*

# Alexander the Great

*Macedonian king*

*Born 356 B.C.,
Pella, Macedonia, in present-day
Balkan Peninsula*

*Died 323 B.C.,
Babylon, in present-day Iraq/Persian
Gulf region*

Alexander was one of the greatest generals in history. When he was twenty years old, he took over his father's kingdom in Macedon. Immediately, he over-powered neighboring tribes that questioned his ability to rule. He then marched his army against the Persian Empire, his kingdom's long-time enemy to the east. But Alexander didn't stop there. He kept marching his army eastward, claiming more and more land. When he was finished, the vast area under his control spread east from Greece to the Himalaya Mountains in northern India. Today, this region is made up of well over a dozen countries. No single king before him had conquered such a great tract of land.

The ancient kingdom of Macedon compares roughly with the modern country of Macedonia, located on the northern border of Greece. When Alexander's father, Philip II, came to power in 359 B.C., the kingdom was weak and disorganized. But Philip strengthened its economy and its military. In fact, through years of constant training and battle, he made the

*"For five years he wandered through the strange, half-known countries of his immense empire."*

army a nearly unbeatable force. Eventually, Philip and his army brought the great Greek city-states of Athens, Sparta, and Thebes under Macedonian rule. Forming this army was the greatest accomplishment of his rule and the greatest gift he could have left his son.

Olympias, Alexander's mother, also gave Alexander something that might have helped spark his desire for conquest. Because she was fond of Greek culture and education, she had the famous Greek philosopher Aristotle tutor her son. She also encouraged Alexander's beliefs in the ancient Greek gods and myths. He spent his childhood dreaming of becoming a conquering hero like Achilles in the *Iliad,* the epic tale of the Trojan war written by the Greek poet Homer. These epic tales stayed with him all of his life. Through his empire, he would try to spread what he thought was the glory of Greek civilization.

Belief in heroic warriors, willful gods, and in his own abilities made the young Alexander arrogant and rude. Yet, at the age of 16, he was managing the daily business of his father's kingdom. A year later, he led a section of the Macedonian army to victory in battle. By 336 B.C., after Philip was assassinated, Alexander took over the throne. In order to protect his reign, he killed those who opposed him.

## Quickly Crushes Enemies

Unafraid of Alexander's heavy hand, northern border tribes under Macedonian control rebelled. In the spring of 335 B.C., Alexander's army quickly defeated them. That summer, Thebes expelled the Macedonian troops stationed there. In response, Alexander had his army destroy the city. Six thousand Thebians were killed. After this, no Greek city-state questioned Macedonian rule.

Alexander then decided to renew the war against the Persian Empire, a campaign started by his father. The eastern part of this empire included Asia Minor (present-day Turkey), which is where Alexander began his attack in 334 B.C. His battle tactics were simple and effective: using his army like a spear, he recklessly charged the center of enemy lines. Enemy

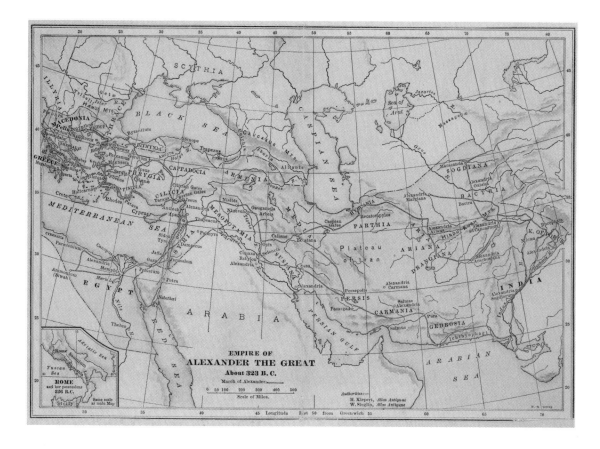

EMPIRE OF
**ALEXANDER THE GREAT**
About 323 B.C.

March of Alexander

0  50 100    200    300    400    500
Scale of Miles.

Authorities:—
H. Kiepert, *Atlas Antiquus*
W. Sieglin, *Atlas Antiquus*

soldiers often ran in confusion. Alexander also used the Macedonian phalanx, a solid block of soldiers arranged in 16 tight rows. With sharp spears sticking out on all sides, this block literally sliced right through the enemy as they charged.

City after city surrendered as Alexander marched his army south. Finally, in the southeast part of Asia Minor, near the ancient city of Issus, Alexander met the emperor Darius III and the main Persian army. Using the phalanx maneuver, Alexander was again victorious. Darius fled, and the entire western Persian Empire was open to Macedonian rule. Alexander, though, proved he was a generous conqueror. He collected taxes from his new subjects in this area, but allowed them to keep their own customs and organizations.

Determined to seize the entire Persian Empire, Alexander destroyed the city of Tyre, the strongest seaport in the area. With it fell Persian naval power in the Mediterranean Sea. In

331 B.C. Alexander sailed to Egypt and easily conquered it. He often founded cities in the areas that he captured, and in Egypt, where the Nile River flowed into the Mediterranean, he founded Alexandria, his greatest city. Meanwhile, Darius had been raising another army in the eastern part of the Empire. Some historians believe that when Darius met Alexander at Gaugamela (an ancient city near the Tigris River in modern Iraq), Darius's army may have numbered almost one million men. But it didn't matter. Alexander shattered Darius's army and his kingship. Darius escaped again, but was murdered ten months later by his own men.

## Calls Himself "Lord of Asia"

With the fall of the centuries-old Persian Empire, Alexander proclaimed himself "Lord of Asia." Led by ambition and curiosity, he set out to explore the empire he had won. Heading east, into what is now Afghanistan, he conquered numerous tribes. He then plunged into India, fighting battles against Indian princes. All were defeated. For five years he wandered through the strange, half-known countries of his immense empire.

Alexander spread Greek culture and learning in the cities he captured and in those he built. He even married Roxana, a Persian princess, in order to secure Asian and Greek cultural ties. But his men soon tired of the endless roaming, and in 326 B.C. they refused to continue. Alexander was forced to cross a vast desert wasteland and return to Babylon, the former capital of the Persian empire. In 323 B.C., while planning a voyage by sea around Arabia, Alexander caught a fever and died at the age of 33. His empire—the largest the world had ever seen to that time—soon vanished, divided among his generals.

# Alfred the Great

*First king of England*
*Born 848*
*Died c. 900*

When the Romans left England in the early fifth century, the people living there—called Britons—were weak and unorganized. Germanic people soon came to this land from the northwest region of modern Germany and the western shores of the Baltic Sea. These tribes—the Angles, the Saxons, and the Jutes—conquered the local Britons and drew them into their own communities. Over the next few centuries, these tribes created a highly cultured society that lasted until the Norman Conquest in 1066 (see **William the Conqueror**). Much of the success of this society has been credited, in fact and in legend, to the wisdom and the talent of the Saxon king Alfred. In English history, he is the only king to have the title "The Great" attached to his name.

When Alfred was born in 848, England was divided into small, independent kingdoms or states. The Angles controlled the northern, central, and eastern areas of the island—Northumbria, Mercia, and East Anglia. The Saxons ruled the southern areas of Essex, Sussex, and Wessex. The Jutes, about

*"In English history, Alfred is the only king to have the title 'The Great' attached to his name."*

whom very little is known, governed the southeastern area of Kent and the Isle of Wight in the English Channel. The term "Anglo-Saxon" was first used to describe Saxons living in England. It separated them from those Saxons who stayed behind on the continent and who were eventually conquered by the Frankish king Charlemagne (see **Charlemagne**). Eventually, the term referred to all the tribes in England, and it is used in this sense here.

Some historians have labeled these Anglo-Saxon kingdoms the heptarchy, a Greek word meaning "seven kingdoms." However, these kingdoms were not very orderly. Their boundaries constantly changed during the seventh and eighth centuries. At one time there may have been 12 kingdoms. And though these tribes were related, they often battled among themselves for land and power.

But the tribes did have one common bond: religion. Late in the sixth century, Pope Gregory (see **Gregory I, the Great**) began a gentle conversion of the Anglo-Saxons to Christianity. It was very successful. All Anglo-Saxons considered themselves members of the same spiritual kingdom, and though each king ruled his own territory, all were loyal to the pope. Many European kings and emperors often sent their sons to the pope to receive his blessing. With this, they hoped their sons would come to lead by "God's grace." That is why the Saxon king of Wessex, Ethelwulf, sent his four-year-old son, Alfred, to Rome. But beside the pope's blessing, young Alfred returned to England the following year with something more: a wonder of the beauty of the architecture, art, and music of Rome. This would greatly fuel his desire to spread learning during his reign as king.

## Vikings Attack Anglo–Saxon Kingdoms

The Anglo-Saxons also had one common enemy: the Vikings, better known as the Danes to the Anglo-Saxons. These fierce warriors came from the Scandinavian lands that later became the modern countries of Denmark, Norway, and Sweden. They began storming the eastern coast of England around the beginning of the ninth century. No one could stop their raids. By the middle of that century, the Danes had overrun almost all the Anglo-Saxon kingdoms. The only kingdom that remained fully free was Wessex, ruled by Alfred's family. But Ethelwulf died in 858, and over the next 12 years, his three eldest sons—Ethelbald, Ethelbert, and Ethelred—each ruled Wessex and tried to defeat the Danes. They all died trying.

In 871 Alfred took control of Wessex and what remained of the other Anglo-Saxon kingdoms. At first, he was able to defend his kingdom against the Danes. But soon they became too powerful. Some historians believe that Alfred then bribed the Danes not to attack for five years. This was a common practice at that time, and might explain why Alfred had time to build up his army and to form his first naval fleet. Whatever the case, the Danes attacked again in 876 and were repelled by Alfred's army.

But two years later, the Danes defeated his army in a surprise attack, and Alfred was forced into hiding at Athelney, an isle surrounded by marshes in southwest England. Just a few months later, however, he rallied his troops and defeated the Dane king Guthrum at Edington in southern England. This victory not only saved Alfred's kingdom, but also prevented England from becoming a Scandinavian country.

## The Viking Age

From roughly the ninth century through the eleventh century, Viking warriors raided the British Isles and the northern coast of Europe seeking land and wealth. They were known by many names: they were called Danes in England, Varangians in Russia, and Norseman or Northmen elsewhere. They were the best sailors and shipbuilders in the world. Their warships—"longboats"—could hold up to 90 men. They were long and narrow, with a high prow (front) and bow (back). Usually at the top of the prow was a carving of a fierce animal head, often that of a dragon. The rest of the longboat was carved and painted, and the warriors' shields hung along the sides. The approach of these warships frightened enemies even before battles had begun. The Vikings also sought adventure, and traveled as far as Greenland and North America.

## Reforms Laws and Learning

In 886 Alfred signed a peace treaty with Guthrum that allowed the Danes to live in the north and east regions of England. This territory became known as the Danelaw. Alfred controlled the Anglo-Saxon regions in the south and west. As king of all the Anglo-Saxons, Alfred developed a system of sensible laws for everyone. He reorganized the army and the finances of his kingdom, and he created the first justice system in which judges traveled around the country.

But the greatest achievement of Alfred's reign was his desire to spread learning. Years of warfare had ruined the system of education, both religious and other. So Alfred, like Charlemagne, gathered together scholars who began court schools. His own children attended, along with children of the nobility, or ruling classes. Even Alfred studied Latin at this time. He then translated several Latin books into Old English, including Pope Gregory's *Pastoral Care* and the Latin Bible, the *Vulgate*. Alfred often put his own thoughts and comments in the many works he translated. Because a series of Danish raids between 892 and 896 were unsuccessful, Alfred was able to spend his final years in peace, devoting time to his writings. After his death around 900, his son Edward the Elder took control of the English throne.

# Attila the Hun

*King of the Huns*
*Born c. 370*
*Died 453*

Very little is known about the origin of the Huns. Sometime in the late fourth century, they poured across Europe like a swarm of locusts. For over two generations, they spread death and destruction. Dressed in their rat-skin hats and foul-smelling leather clothes, the Huns terrified all those who saw them. Wherever they went, they left behind ravaged fields, smoking ruins, and countless dead. The last and most destructive of the Hunnic chieftains was Attila. Many of his victims called him the "scourge of God" because they felt he was sent as punishment for their sins. Under his leadership, his tribe marched into Europe and tried to conquer the Roman Empire. Even though they failed to do so, the Huns changed the way men would do battle for the next 1,500 years.

The earliest historical records show that the Huns came from a region in eastern Asia where the modern countries of Kazakhstan, China, and Mongolia now border. The Huns were a nomadic people: they had no fixed home but roamed about from place to place. They lived by hunting and gathering, and

> *"Many of his victims called him the 'scourge of God' because they felt he was sent as punishment for their sins."*

used flocks of sheep as their traveling supply of food and leather. But they were mostly predators. Since they had no building or manufacturing skills, all their supplies came in the form of booty, or what they could take from their defeated enemies. Often, a weapon that a Hun used came from the body of his most recent victim.

The Huns easily took whatever they wanted as they traveled everywhere by horse. Indeed, the Huns basically lived on horseback, whether eating, drinking, or sleeping. They only dismounted when it was absolutely necessary. As such, they were excellent horsemen, a skill that served them very well in battle. They would come upon their enemies in a fury, making savage noises. Huns often attacked with only a sword or a spear or a short bow. However, speed and courage were the principal weapons of these highly efficient fighters. And they were merciless, taking few prisoners and showing no pity.

## Kills Brother, Made Sole Ruler

Early in the fifth century, the Huns moved into the area of Pannonia, what is now Hungary and eastern Austria. In 434 this tribe of fierce warriors came under the leadership of Attila and his brother Bleda. Attila was born between 370 and 400. Not much is known about his character other than he was strong and his followers were devoted to him. A weak ruler did not live very long in Hunnic culture, and Attila led the Huns for 19 years. He was also very ruthless: in 445 he killed his brother and became sole ruler of the Huns.

One of Attila's first moves as king of the Huns was to establish his strength over the Eastern Roman Empire. Because of a previous peace treaty, the Eastern Empire was supposed to pay the Huns an annual tribute of 350 pounds of gold. It had not paid this tribute for several years, however, so Attila demanded that the amount be doubled. The Empire agreed. But in 441, while the Eastern Empire was defending Roman-controlled Egypt against the Vandals (a Germanic tribe), Attila broke the peace treaty. He attacked and destroyed the weakened Roman forts and cities along the Danube River in present-day southern Germany. He soon negotiated another peace treaty with the Empire. This time, however, he tripled the tribute to 2,100 pounds of gold a year.

In 450 the new Eastern emperor, Marcian, refused to continue paying Attila his tribute. The Western emperor, Valentinian III, also rejected Attila's demand for a tribute. Attila then claimed Princess Honoria, Valentinian's sister, as his wife. When his claim was rejected, he pushed his tribe against the Western Empire. The Huns cut a path of destruction along the Rhine Valley and entered into Gaul, what is now France and Belgium. Here Attila met two forces: those of Aetius (a Roman general who had been Attila's friend) and those of Theodoric (king of the Visigoths, a Germanic tribe the Huns battled before). The fighting was fierce and Theodoric was killed, but the Huns suffered badly. They were forced to retreat from Gaul. This was Attila's first—and only—defeat.

## Attacks Romans in Revenge

In the spring of 452, seeking revenge against the Romans, the Huns attacked and destroyed several northern Italian cities and towns. They then prepared to march to Rome. But they soon withdrew from Italy because famine and disease were spreading throughout the country. Some historians also believe Pope Leo I had met with Attila and asked him to leave Italy. Since Attila had a high regard for holy men, he agreed to the pope's wish.

The following year an aging Attila (who already had many wives) married a young Hunnish woman named Ildico. Attila drank excessively at the wedding feast. By the end of the night, he collapsed on his bed. Frequently, Attila suffered from nose bleeds, especially after drinking. This night had been no exception. Because he was too drunk to wake up, however, he literally drowned in his own blood. Like other chieftains of that time, Attila was secretly buried; to this day his burial site has never been found. His numerous sons divided his empire, and the Huns soon were no longer a force. But the memory of the Huns superior horsemanship in battle remained. For centuries, men would copy their fierce fighting style.

# Augustus

*First Roman emperor*

*Born September 23, 63 B.C.,
Rome, in present-day Italy*

*Died August 19, A.D. 14,
Nola, Campania*

*"His creation of the lasting Roman Empire out of this scattered republic was the work of a political genius."*

For centuries, the old Roman Republic had expanded by claiming territories around it. But it could never completely control these lands as a single unit. When Augustus became master of the Roman world, he placed the various territories under his absolute rule. His creation of the lasting Roman Empire out of this scattered republic was the work of a political genius. Even though he was cold and ambitious and ruled the Empire like a dictator, he listened to the opinions and the wishes of the Roman citizens. He never openly abused the ideals and traditions that Rome held dear, and his encouragement of writing and the arts helped label the time of his rule the Golden Age of Roman Civilization.

Born Caius Octavius (Octavian) in 63 B.C., he was only four when his father died. His mother's uncle, the famous Roman general and dictator Julius Caesar (see **Julius Caesar**), helped raise him. Octavian was 18 and studying in Greece when Caesar was assassinated in 44 B.C. He quickly returned to Rome after learning through Caesar's will that he had been made Caesar's son and heir. Marc Antony, a friend of Caesar, was then consul (manager of the city) and was becoming all-powerful. Members of the Senate, Rome's governing body, soon plotted against Antony, so he escaped to Cisalpine Gaul (what is now northern Italy) where he controlled part of the Roman army. The Senate then made Octavian commander of the army and sent him after Antony. Octavian defeated Antony at the battle of Mutina (present-day city of Modena), but Antony escaped to the south of Gaul (France). Together with Marcus Aemilius Lepidus, the governor of that province, Antony raised a new army.

Octavian did not want a civil war to ruin Rome, so he convinced the Senate in 43 B.C. to allow Antony, Lepidus, and him to govern the Empire for five years. This Second Triumvirate (a triumvirate is a ruling group of three; the first had been formed by Caesar) immediately tracked down and killed anyone connected to the murder of Caesar. Friction soon arose in the three-way partnership, and in 40 B.C. the triumvirs decided to divide the Roman world between them: Octavian received Europe, Antony the East, and Lepidus the African provinces. They ruled this way until the end of their designated five years, in 38 B.C. Octavian then arranged to have the triumvirate renewed for yet another five years, but the partnership was falling apart.

Lepidus was weak and gradually lost his role in this government. Octavian and Antony, suspicious of each other, soon became rivals. Seeking more power, Antony married Cleopatra (see **Cleopatra VII**), queen of the independent country of Egypt. He intended to rule both his portion of the Empire and Egypt with Cleopatra. This was not only an offense against the Roman Empire but an insult to Octavian as well: Antony was also married to Octavian's sister Octavia. In 31 B.C. Octavian attacked and defeated the forces of Antony and Cleopatra in a great sea battle near Actium in Greece. Afterward, Antony and Cleopatra committed suicide. Egypt became a Roman province, and Octavian became sole ruler of the widening Roman world.

## Octavian Becomes Augustus

Rome was at peace. Octavian did not want any more civil wars to erupt, so he gave up his extraordinary powers in 28

B.C., choosing to remain only a consul. The following year, he offered to step down completely, but the grateful Senate offered him many positions and titles. They gave him supreme power for ten years and granted him the title of *augustus,* "reverend." And he was made *princeps,* "first citizen or President of the Republic." To honor him, the Senate even changed the name of the eighth month on the calendar to August. Although Augustus, as he was called thereafter, did not accept many of the titles awarded him, he accepted the positions the Senate had given him and crafted a new form of government.

Gathering the power of his political positions together, Augustus gradually developed what became the office of the Roman emperor. The emperor was not a king since there was no guarantee that his relatives would succeed him in that position. The Senate, the army, and the people of Rome had to approve of a person becoming emperor. But like a king, Augustus came to possess every power imaginable. On the surface, the government seemed to be controlled by the Senate and looked like a republic. Underneath, however, it was a virtual monarchy as Augustus directed the workings of the government and the army and arranged for his position to remain in his family.

## Rome Thrives Under Rule

Augustus was not a hungry king or dictator: he ruled the Roman Empire generously. He kept a careful watch over the outlying provinces, but allowed them to run their own local governments. For being able to freely maintain their ethnic cultures and customs, people in these provinces were grateful to Augustus and did not question his rule. At home he used his enormous power for the advancement of Rome and its citizens. With peace throughout the Empire, trade increased and many people in the lower classes became rich. Augustus helped the economy by organizing a census and making taxation more fair. He also made Rome safe by forming fire and police forces and by improving its system of roads.

Eventually, Augustus rebuilt Rome. He erected numerous temples in the city and restored dozens of others. Among the most magnificent ones he built were the Forum of Augustus, with its temple of Mars the Avenger and its 108 statues, and the Temple of Apollo, with a Greek and Latin library built on either side of its entrance. But architects and sculptors were not the only artists Augustus favored. Many great men of letters prospered under Augustus's support, including the historian Livy and the poets Horace, Ovid, and Virgil.

For over 40 years Augustus ruled the Empire as the *pater patriae,* "father of the fatherland." His health declined in his later years, and he died in A.D. 14 after catching a chill while sailing at night outside Nola in the Campania region of southern Italy. The title of *imperator* (emperor), commander of the army, passed on to his stepson, Tiberius.

# Julius Caesar

*Roman general and dictator*

*Born July 13, c. 100 B.C.,
Rome, present-day Italy*

*Died March 15, 44 B.C.,
Rome*

*"Controlling almost
every aspect of Roman
life, he soon thought
himself almost
godlike."*

A brilliant general and statesman, Julius Caesar brought about the end of the Roman Republic. For almost 500 years, Rome had been ruled by a few powerful men at a time. This ended when Caesar gained control and became Rome's sole master. He was eventually murdered because people thought he wanted to become king, and they feared his lasting influence. At his death, however, he had already laid the foundations for an empire that would rule Greek and Roman society for centuries. Although the Roman empire has long since passed into history, for almost 2,000 years his name has remained, used as a title for those in power—"Caesar" for ancient Roman emperors, "Kaiser" for German leaders, "Czar" for Russian rulers.

Caesar's full name was Gaius Julius Caesar. He was born into the Julians, one of the oldest patrician (upper-class) families in Rome. This family was not celebrated for either military or political accomplishments, but it held some status in Rome: Caesar's father was a member of the Senate, Rome's governing body. Because of this, Caesar received an excellent education, especially in the Greek and Latin arts of rhetoric (speech making). His way into politics was opened when his aunt married the Roman consul Gaius Marius. (Consuls were elected officials who acted almost like presidents, managing the city and controlling its army.) Although part of the nobility, both Marius and Caesar were members of the democratic or popular party. To secure his position within this political group, which controlled the government then, Caesar married Cornelia in 84 B.C. She was the daughter of Lucius Cornelius Cinna, another consul and leader of the popular party.

In 82 B.C., during a brief civil war, leaders of this governing party were removed from office. The conservative party of landowners came to power and Rome fell under the control of the dictator Sulla. Trying to weaken the ties in the popular party, Sulla order Caesar to divorce Cornelia. But Caesar refused and had to flee Rome in 81 B.C. to escape the dictator's threats. Three years later, after Sulla's death, Caesar returned to Rome to begin his political career.

With his gift for rhetoric, Caesar called for improvements in the government to help the common citizen. These actions earned him the popularity of the people; they also earned him the hatred of the mostly conservative Senate. But Caesar, in addition to being intelligent, was crafty. He liked living in luxury, and he gave expensive gifts to his friends. He also was not afraid to offer bribes to the officials and the voters of Rome in order to secure a position in the Roman government. Beginning in 69 B.C. he was elected to numerous positions, from praetor (judge) to governor of the Roman-controlled province of Farther Spain.

## Uses Partnership to Gain Power

Along the way, Caesar allied himself with Marcus Lucinius Crassus, the wealthiest man in Rome, who helped Caesar pay off his many debts. He also sought out Gnaeus Pompeius Magnus (Pompey), commander of the Roman army, who had recently returned to Rome a hero after conquering much land in the East. Caesar knew Crassus and Pompey shared two qualities: each wanted control in the government and each was suspicious of the other. Knowing they could help him win rule of the Roman state; Caesar convinced Cassus and Pompey to put aside their differences and join with him in a political alliance. They agreed, and the three partners became known as the First Triumvirate (a triumvirate is a commission of three partners).

With Crassus's power and Pompey's prestige behind him, Caesar was elected consul in 59 B.C. He helped pass legislation that met both men's needs. In return, he received the governorships of three Roman provinces: Illyricum (the western shore of the modern Balkan Peninsula), Cisalpine Gaul (now northern Italy), and Transalpine Gaul (southeastern France). Now controlling the armies in these areas, Caesar sought more power. Beginning in 58 B.C., he attacked Gaul (France and Belgium) and fought Gallic tribes, pushing them north to the English Channel. Twice he invaded Britain. By 51 B.C. Caesar had brought the Gallic tribes under Roman control.

But the triumvirate was coming apart. Crassus had been killed in 53 B.C. while leading an army against Parthia (an ancient country in modern northeast Iran). Pompey had been made sole consul in 52 B.C. Jealous of Caesar's success and rising popularity, he plotted with the Senate against Caesar. In December of 50 B.C., the Senate commanded Caesar to disband his army and return to Rome a private citizen. He refused. On January 10, 49 B.C., he led his army across the Rubicon, a shallow river separating Cisalpine Gaul from Italy, and marched toward Rome. His partnership with Pompey came to an end; civil war had begun.

## "I Came, I Saw, I Conquered"
Pompey and his army fled Rome. After ruling the city as dictator for 11 days, Caesar had the people elect him consul. He then moved against Pompey, defeating his army at Pharsalus in northern Greece. Pompey escaped to Egypt, only to be murdered. Having followed him there, Caesar became involved in a dispute between Ptolemy XII and his sister Cleopatra (see **Cleopatra VII**) over who would rule Egypt.

Caesar, captivated by Cleopatra, defeated her brother's forces and placed her on the throne. A rebellion in Syria by Pompey's ally Pharnaces soon pulled Caesar and his army away from Egypt. His victory there was swift, and he reported back to Rome: *"Veni, vidi, vici"* ("I came, I saw, I conquered").

Without a rival, Caesar was in complete control. In 46 B.C. he was appointed dictator for ten years. Two years later, he was made dictator for life, a position no one before had held. For all purposes, the Roman Republic had come to an end. Caesar's first reforms as ruler showed he could be compassionate and generous. He pardoned all his enemies, improved housing for the poor, granted Roman citizenship to outsiders, and increased the number of members in the Senate, making it more reflective of Rome's populace. He even corrected the calendar, and had the month of July named after him.

These reforms secured Caesar's position. Controlling almost every aspect of Roman life, he soon thought himself almost godlike. Members of the Senate, both Caesar's opponents and friends, feared he was becoming an absolute king and plotted his assassination. In 44 B.C., on the Ides of March (the 15th), Caesar entered the Senate and was set upon by his attackers. Using daggers, they stabbed him 23 times. He fell dead at the foot of the statue of Pompey, his former partner and rival. His enemies had removed Caesar, but they could not reverse the course he had set for Rome. His adopted son and heir, the future Augustus (see **Augustus**), would strengthen this coming empire, and it would last for almost 500 years.

# Canute I, the Great

*Viking king of England, Denmark, and Norway*

*Born c. 995*

*Died November 12, 1035, Shaftesbury, England*

*"For the first time since the Romans left England in the early fifth century the entire country came under one ruler, and his name was Canute."*

For almost 100 years after the reign of Alfred the Great (see **Alfred the Great**), the English (Anglo-Saxons) and the Danes (Vikings) lived side by side in England. The Danes were confined to regions in northeast England called the Danelaw, while the English controlled the rest of the country. But it was an uneasy arrangement. Although marriages occurred between the two peoples, their relationship was more often violent: both sought land the other owned.

In 975 Ethelred II was crowned king of England. He was neither a good warrior nor a capable king, and any bond that remained between the English and the Danes soon disappeared. Beginning around 980, the Danes began raiding Ethelred's kingdom. They continued to do so for almost the next 35 years. Then a Dane rose to conquer England and unite the English and the Danish. For the first time since the Romans left England in the early fifth century, the entire country came under one ruler, and his name was Canute.

Canute was born around 995 in the midst of these raids.

His father, Sweyn Haraldson, was king of Denmark; his mother, Gunhild, was a Polish princess. Not much is known about Canute's childhood. He must have had training in fighting battles, though, for in 1013, while still young, he accompanied his father on attacks on England. That year, Sweyn captured almost all of the country, forcing Ethelred to flee to his brother-in-law's duchy (territory ruled by a duke) in Normandy, a region in modern northwest France.

Early in 1014, however, Sweyn died. Harald, Sweyn's oldest son, then became king of Denmark, while the Danish army in England declared Canute king of England. But Ethelred soon returned to England with a large army, driving Canute back to Denmark. The Danes lost control of the Danelaw. In the fall of 1015 Canute led his army to reconquer England. He soon captured the states of Wessex and Northumbria. He was planning his attack on London when Ethelred died suddenly in April of 1016. Edmund Ironside, Ethelred's son, continued his father's fight.

## Becomes Sole King of England

But Edmund was no match for Canute. On October 18, 1016, he led his army against the Danes at Assandun (modern Ashingdun). Canute beat him soundly, then forced him to sign a peace treaty. The treaty gave Edmund control over the state of Wessex, while Canute received control over the rest of England. The two rulers then exchanged oaths of friendship. But this dual rule of England did not last long. Edmund died in November, and all the nobles of England recognized Canute as the sole king of England.

The country was now at peace. Recognizing this, Canute did not want to disturb the social order. He tried to maintain English traditions. He used early English laws as models for new ones he developed, and he built his government using both English and Danish nobles. Seeking good relations with the Church, he rebuilt many monasteries and churches and supported others with money. Hoping to strengthen his position with the English people, Canute married Emma, the widow of Ethelred, in July 1017. His son by this marriage, Harthacanute, would succeed him to the English throne.

In the summer of 1018, Canute's brother Harald died without leaving an heir. Canute now became sole king of Denmark. In 1019 he traveled to his home country to secure his rule there. It was difficult for Canute to rule in both countries at the same time, so in some areas he divided the governing power among nobles and in others he left complete control of the government in the hands of a regent (person who controls a government when the ruler is absent). This system came to haunt him. Canute had to make many trips between England and Denmark to protect his rule against plots and revolts in both countries.

## Becomes Most Powerful Northern Ruler

Despite these problems, Canute sought to widen his rule. In 1015 the country of Norway had been under the control of Canute's brother, Eric. That same year Eric left Norway to help Canute in his battles with Ethelred, leaving the throne unprotected. The following year Olaf the Stout took control of it. By 1023 Eric was dead, and Canute had gained some control over his two kingdoms.

Canute then claimed he was the rightful heir to the Norwegian throne. Olaf disagreed. Canute finally moved his army against Olaf in September 1026, only to be beaten at the mouth of the Holy River. But before attacking Olaf, Canute had bribed Norwegian nobles to turn against the Norwegian king. His plot worked. Rebellious nobles forced Olaf to flee to Russia. In 1028 Canute easily advanced through the Norwegian kingdom and took the crown.

That same year Canute called an imperial meeting at Trondheim, then the capital of Norway. It was the only time in Canute's life that the nobles from all three parts of his kingdom met. He created a system of earls, regents, and advisors to help run his vast realm. In the beginning things ran smoothly, and Canute was able to return to England in 1029 with his kingdom secure. But soon problems developed—his Anglo-Danish Empire was just too large for one man to rule easily. By 1033 Norwegian nobles complained that Canute's regents ruled too harshly. They threatened to bring Olaf back to power.

Canute never had the chance to stop any rebellion. He died in England on November 12, 1035. His 19-year reign of peace over England had come to an end. His son Harthacanute ruled briefly as king of the entire realm, but he did not last long. By 1040 the Anglo-Danish Empire was an idea of the past, and in 1042 Edward the Confessor (son of Ethelred) claimed the English throne.

# Catherine II, the Great

*Russian empress*

*Born April 21, 1729,
Anhalt-Zerbst (modern Germany)*

*Died November 6, 1796,
St. Petersburg, Russia*

*"Only her writings about the theory of government were enlightened, never her actions in governing."*

Just before her death, Catherine the Great asked that her gravestone bear the following message: "When she ascended the throne of Russia, she wished to do good and tried to bring happiness, freedom, and prosperity to her subjects." It is fitting these words never marked her stone. For although she brought great power and glory to Russia, it was not shared by all the people in her country. She wished to rule Russia as an "enlightened despot," or a ruler who governs with absolute power for the good of the people. But only her *writings* about the theory of government were enlightened, never her *actions* in governing. In the end, she was admired by the wealthy of her country and despised by its lower classes.

Catherine was born a German princess, the daughter of Christian August, who was the prince of Anhalt-Zerbst. Her birth name was Sophia, and she spent her childhood in Stettin, a city in Prussia (what is now Germany). There she learned to speak both French and German. Although her parents did not control vast lands and wealth, her mother's family was well connected with some of the great royal families in Europe. At the age of fourteen, Sophia was taken by her mother to Russia to be wed to Grand Prince Peter Fyodorovich, heir to the Russian throne. (Throughout history, sons and daughters were often married off to secure treaties and associations between nations.) Before her marriage, Sophia converted to the Orthodox religion of Russia and became known by her Russian name, Catherine.

Catherine's married life was unhappy. Peter was mentally unstable, and he was unfaithful. In response, Catherine also took lovers. This led many people at the time to question whether Paul, her first born, was actually the son of Peter. But Catherine was ambitious—she had plans of taking the Russian crown herself—so she accepted her marriage on the surface. She easily adapted to Russian ways and learned the language as quickly as possible, even getting up in the middle of the night to memorize her lessons. She also began reading the works of the major European thinkers of that time, and was especially drawn to the philosophical movement known as the Enlightenment (see **Thomas Jefferson**). This movement insisted that life should be based on reason, or logic, and not on old customs. All people were entitled to certain civil rights, and it was the duty of governments to protect these rights. These ideas began to shape Catherine's political thinking.

## Catherine Seizes Power

In 1762 Peter succeeded to the throne as Czar Peter III ("Czar" was the Russian word for "Caesar"). But his personality and his political decisions angered many Russians, especially the nobility, or ruling classes. In the meantime, Catherine was becoming increasingly popular. With the army's help, she managed a coup d'état (overthrow of the government). Paul was the rightful heir, or successor, to the throne, but Catherine had herself crowned Empress of Russia. Peter was imprisoned, then murdered a few days later.

Catherine immediately set about reforming old Russian laws. She labored tirelessly, often rising at five or six in the morning and then working for 15 hours. During her first years on the throne, she wrote down her ideas for a model Russian government, which she published in 1767 as the *Instruction*. This document clearly shows Enlightenment thinking, traits it would come to share with America's Declaration of Independence and Constitution, written about ten years later. In this document, Catherine stated that government officials must act morally, and they must rule according to the desires of the people. She also wrote that land can be best farmed or developed by men who are free and who own that land.

This last belief seemed to contradict Russia's long-held system of serfdom, or the practice of forcing peasant farmers (serfs) to work on land owned by the nobility. Serfs were treated like slaves, often being bought and sold at auctions in public squares. Some were even traded for dogs or gambled away. To change this, Catherine called together representatives from all social classes in Russia (except the serfs). She wanted them to discuss the needs of the country and to use the *Instruction* to simplify Russia's laws. But they could agree on nothing, so the old laws and practices remained unchanged.

Many people in countries throughout Europe read the *Instruction*, and Catherine was widely praised as a true "enlightened despot." But her views on the function of government soon changed. Because she had usurped (took over wrongfully by force) the Russian throne with the help of the nobility, she could not afford to anger them. Therefore, she could not govern all of her subjects equally. She had to favor the nobility in order to keep their support. Catherine freed them from required government service, as either civil servants or soldiers. She also freed them from paying taxes, and gave them complete control over their land and serfs. This angered the serfs, who rebelled at least 60 times during Catherine's rule. Protecting the interests of the nobility, she crushed each revolt.

## Captures Lands, Extends Empire

While Catherine strengthened her power at home, she also sought to increase it in Europe. She believed that the greater the population, the greater the might of the Russian Empire. Trying to add to the size of her empire, she gained influence over the king of neighboring Poland, and then defeated that country when it rebelled in 1768. Over the next 20 years, along with the leaders of Austria and Prussia, Catherine seized large portions of Poland. In 1792, Poland no longer existed on the map. She also took control of the Black Sea and the Crimea (part of present-day Ukraine) by defeating Turkey. When Catherine took over Russia, she ruled about 20 million people. When she finished extending the borders of the Russian Empire, she controlled over 36 million people.

Catherine's reign was a mixture of opposites. She forced serfs to live under terrible conditions, yet she introduced many remarkable steps for the care of the sick and of the needy. She founded hospitals and even promoted the new medical practice of vaccination. She also attached a great importance to education and to the arts. She formed schools and encouraged artists and playwrights, even writing a few plays herself. Nevertheless, her attempt to bring high culture to Russian society was offset by her desire for extravagant feasts and parties. When she died from a stroke in 1796, leaving the throne to Paul, her court was as culturally rich as any in Europe. Unfortunately, only a few of her countrymen could enjoy it: the lower classes of Russia remained poor.

# Charlemagne

*King of the Franks*
*Born c. 742*
*Died January 28, 814*

*"His creation of this ordered empire made him perhaps one of the greatest leaders in the West since Julius Caesar."*

On Christmas Day in the year 800, Charles the Great, king of the Franks, was praying during service in the great cathedral of St. Peter in Rome. He had come to Rome to support Pope Leo III, whom the Romans had threatened to remove from the papacy, or office of the pope. When Charles rose from kneeling near the high altar, the pope produced a crown and placed it upon Charles's head. The people in the church cried out, "To Charles Augustus, crowned by God, great and peace-giving emperor, life and victory." Now Charles—better known as Charlemagne, the old French version of Charles the Great—added the territory of the former West Roman Empire in Europe to his vast kingdom united by a common faith. His creation of this ordered empire made him one of the greatest leaders in the West since Julius Caesar (see **Julius Caesar**).

Charlemagne was born around 742. Not much is known about his childhood. He spent much time horseback riding and hunting, common activities of medieval nobility, of which he was a part. Also common during the Middle Ages was the lack of reading and writing skills among everyone except members of the Church. Charlemagne was no exception. And like many during that time, he was raised a devout Christian. Both of these traits—his religion and his lack of schooling—would figure prominently during his future rule.

The Roman Empire had given way in Western Europe almost 300 years before Charlemagne's birth. So-called Germanic states now controlled this area. One of the most important of these was that of the Franks, a people who controlled the Rhineland region (what is now western Germany and eastern France). The Franks were ruled by kings, but real power in the kingdom was wielded by the Mayor of the Palace. This position had been held by Charlemagne's grandfather, Charles Martel, and his father, Pepin the Short.

Since the time of Pope Gregory I (see **Gregory I, the Great**), the power of the Catholic Church grew throughout the kingdoms in Europe. Charlemagne's family, the Carolingians, had always been supported by the Church. So Pepin the Short used the influence of Pope Zacharias to have the Frank king, Childeric, removed in 751. He then had himself declared king. When he died 17 years later, his two sons, Charlemagne and Carloman, became joint kings.

The two brothers did not get along, and this threatened to tear the kingdom apart. But the Frankish state was saved when Carloman died unexpectedly in 771. Charlemagne became sole ruler of the Franks, inheriting his brother's portion of the kingdom. Like his ancestors, Charlemagne was a warrior, and he naturally desired to conquer more lands. In 773 he decided to help the pope defend Rome against the Lombards, a Germanic tribe that had settled in northern Italy. After three years of battles, Charlemagne was victorious and brought that Italian region under his control. It was the beginning of his close association with the papacy.

## Warrior for Christianity

Since he was a Christian ruler, Charlemagne felt it was his duty to spread his faith. Beginning in 772, he led a crusade

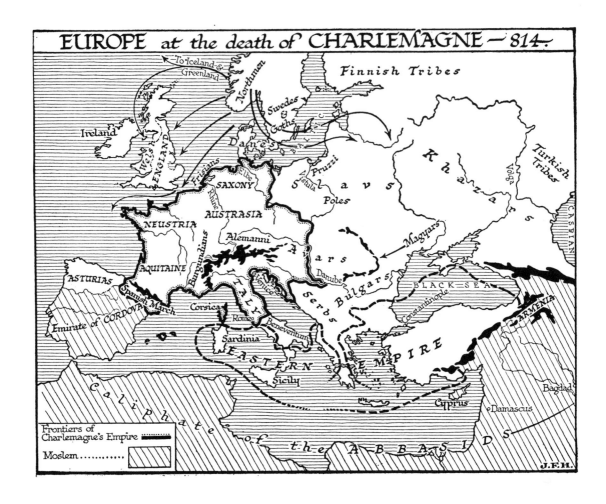

EUROPE at the death of CHARLEMAGNE — 814.

Frontiers of Charlemagne's Empire ........
Moslem ............

against the Saxons, a tribe that often attacked Frankish borders. Related to the tribes that settled in southern England some 300 years before, these Saxons occupied a region in what is now northwest Germany. As they were not Christians, Charlemagne sought to conquer them not only to protect his kingdom but to save their souls. During his first campaign against them, he destroyed Irminsul, the sacred tree that was the symbol of old Saxon religion.

The war raged on until 804, when the Saxons could no longer resist and became part of the Frankish realm. These campaigns showed Charlemagne's skill as a leader and his strong desire to spread Christianity. But they also showed him to be ruthless: he forced both conversions (of religion) and baptisms with the sword. And during one battle in 782, he had some 5,000 Saxons beheaded.

After the Saxons, Charlemagne conquered other tribes in northern Europe. But he also suffered defeat. In 778 he attacked the Muslims in Spain. The rear guard of his army, commanded by Roland, was ambushed and defeated by Basque warriors (Basques were independent people living on either side of the Pyrenees, mountains on the French-Spanish border). This battle became a legend and was the subject of the French epic poem *Chanson de Roland* (*Song of Roland*), written during the eleventh century.

## Brings About Renaissance of Learning

The spread of Christianity was not Charlemagne's only interest. Perhaps driven by his own poor education, he also wanted a renaissance, or rebirth, of learning and knowledge to sweep through his kingdom. In the 780s and 790s, he called to his court the leading scholars in Europe. Even though they set up schools, their main concern was to translate old texts and copy manuscripts (books had to be copied by hand until around 1500). Without their effort, almost all the great works of classical literature would be unknown today. These scholars also reformed handwriting. The script used then was almost illegible—letters ran into one another. A new form was developed in which the letters and words were separated. Modern lower-case letters derive from this form.

The climax of Charlemagne's reign was his crowning by Pope Leo III as Roman emperor. At first, it was only a symbol of his control over Western Europe. But the Byzantine Empire (East Roman Empire) viewed his taking of this title as a challenge to their authority. It was not until 813, after a series a battles and negotiations between the two, that the Empire finally accepted his use of this title. That same year, after having ruled as king of the Franks for 46 years and as emperor of the Romans for 13 years, Charlemagne passed the crown to his son, Louis.

Charlemagne died from pneumonia in 814, hoping his kingdom—and a united Europe—would endure for ages. It did not. His grandsons, inheriting the kingdom from their father, fought among themselves. They finally negotiated a peace and signed the Treaty of Verdun in 843. It split Charlemagne's powerful Frankish kingdom into regions that eventually became the modern nations of Western Europe.

# Charles V

*Spanish king and Holy Roman emperor*

*Born February 24, 1500,*
*Ghent, the Netherlands*

*Died September 21, 1558,*
*San Jeronimo de Yuste, Spain*

Charles V was ruler of one of the largest empires in the history of the world. It spread east from Spain to include the kingdoms of Germany, Hungary, Bohemia, Naples, and Sicily, and it spread south and west to include possessions in North Africa and the Americas. Ruling these vast and different territories for 40 years, he dominated European and world politics. But Charles, a Catholic, was not powerful enough to stop the German religious reformer Martin Luther (see **Martin Luther**) and the ultimate spread of Protestantism. His successes in the Americas kept Spain at the top of world power for 100 years, but the building of his fortunes in the New World—led by his *conquistadors* (conquerors)—forever erased the empires of the native Aztec and Inca.

Charles was born in the Netherlands in 1500. He was the son of Philip I, duke of Burgundy, and Joanna, queen of Castile. Joanna, the daughter of Spanish rulers Isabella I and Ferdinand II (see **Isabella I and Ferdinand II**), suffered from a mental illness. So when Philip died in 1506, Charles was raised by his

> "Ruling these vast and different territories for 40 years, Charles dominated European and world politics.

aunt, Margaret of Austria. As a boy, he enjoyed hunting, music, singing, art, and architecture. When he turned 15, he became ruler of the Netherlands. Just a year later, when his grandfather Ferdinand II died, he inherited Spain and its empire.

Charles traveled to Spain in 1517 to assume the rule there, but he was still very young. He knew neither the language nor the customs of his Spanish subjects, and he surrounded himself with Flemish advisors. This angered many people in Spain. Two years later, he bribed the electors in the Holy Roman Empire to gain election as the new Holy Roman emperor, succeeding his grandfather Maximilian I. This angered French king Francis I and English king Henry VIII, both of whom wanted to be the new emperor. Thus began a rivalry among the three young kings (especially between Charles and Francis) that was to last for the rest of their lives.

## Begins Fight Against Reformation

When Charles was only 17, a German monk named Martin Luther nailed a list of 95 complaints against the Catholic Church on the door of a church in Wittenberg, Germany. This began a movement in Europe that came to known as the Protestant Reformation. Charles, raised a devout Catholic, paid little attention to Luther over the next few years and the movement spread. Finally, in 1521, however, Charles and an assembly of German princes, called a Diet, summoned Luther to the German town of Worms, demanding he change his views. But Luther refused, and Charles and the Diet declared him an outlaw of the Church. This did little to stop Luther, who escaped punishment and continued to state his views.

Charles could not keep a check on Luther because he had to focus his attention on a war with France over Italy. Known as the Italian Wars, battles between Spain and France had been fought since the beginning of the century over rich and divided territories in Italy. In 1521 Charles invaded areas in northern Italy controlled by France. Already humiliated by Charles, Francis I angrily fought back, but in 1525 Charles defeated Francis at the battle of Pavia, captured him, and then held him prisoner for a year. After his release Francis again opposed

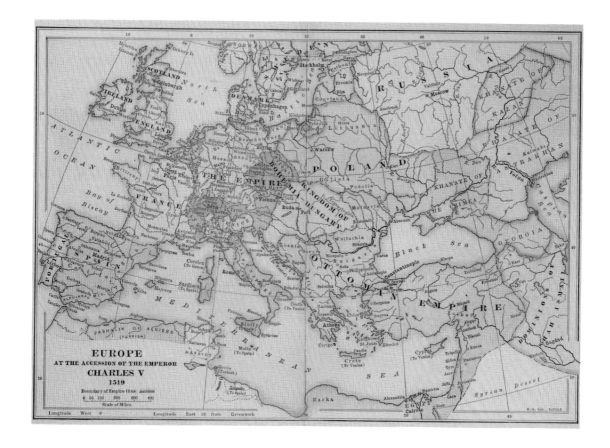

EUROPE
AT THE ACCESSION OF THE EMPEROR
CHARLES V
1519
Boundary of Empire thus:
0   50  100     200      300      400
Scale of Miles.

Spanish control in Italy, joining with Henry VIII and Pope Clement VII. But Charles's imperial forces, gathered from his vast empire, were too strong. They brutally attacked Rome in 1527; Francis, Henry, and the pope were forced to recognize Charles's position in Italy. In 1530 Clement VII crowned Charles Holy Roman emperor at Bologna, Italy.

## Gains Riches From the Americas

While Charles had been securing his empire in Western Europe, his military generals, the conquistadors, had been winning tremendous lands and wealth in the Americas. In Mexico, Hernán Cortés led Spanish forces against the ancient Aztec empire. He marched his army through Mexico in 1519 to the Aztec capital of Tenochtitlán (modern Mexico City). Sitting on horses in their gleaming armor, the Spaniards looked like gods to the Aztec. Moctezuma II, the Aztec ruler (see **Moctezuma II**), gave gifts of gold and silver as peace offerings. But Cortés wanted more treasures, and over the next two years he massacred the Aztec, finally destroying Tenochtitlán in 1521. Even more ruthless than Cortés was Francisco Pizarro. Landing in Peru in 1532 with a small Spanish army, Pizarro first befriended then captured the Inca emperor, Atahualpa. After receiving a tremendous ransom for the emperor's release, Pizarro murdered Atahualpa, then claimed the Inca empire for Spain, killing all the Inca who did not cooperate.

For the remainder of his reign, Charles had to fight to secure his empire. Turks from the Ottoman Empire, based in present-day Turkey, challenged Charles's authority in the Mediterranean and in Central Europe. The Turks first killed the king of Hungary and Bohemia in 1526, but Charles, a member of the Habsburg family, inherited those kingdoms. The Turks, however, proceeded to threaten Europe, so Charles met them in battle in 1529 and again in 1532. He captured the Turkish stronghold at Tunis (city in present-day Tunisia in northern Africa) in 1535. The Turks did not give up, continuing to attack the Italian coast. After suffering a defeat in 1541 at a Turkish base in Algiers in northern Africa, Charles had to sign a truce with the Ottoman Empire.

After the truce, Charles tried to restore Catholic unity to his empire. In response, German Protestant princes formed an alliance known as the Schmalkaldic League. Under the protection of the League, the Reformation spread through most of Germany. Charles's imperial army met this league in Germany in 1547 at the battle of Muhlberg. Although the forces of the German princes were destroyed, the idea behind the Reformation was strong enough to carry on. Charles's empire would never be fully Catholic.

By 1556 Charles's reign was over. Having grown tired of running his vast empire, he abdicated (resigned the crown). The majority of his empire went to his son Philip II. The lands controlled by the Habsburg family and the title of Holy Roman emperor went to his younger brother, Ferdinand I. Charles retired to a monastery in Spain where, on September 21, 1558, he died clutching a crucifix.

# Winston Churchill

*English statesman and writer*

*Born November 30, 1874,*
*Oxfordshire, England*

*Died January 24, 1965,*
*London, England*

When he was in school, Winston Churchill did so poorly in mathematics and in the ancient languages of Greek and Latin that he was considered a dunce. The only subject in which he showed any ability was English. The one thing he learned best of all, as he later said, was the "essential structure of the ordinary English sentence—which is a noble thing." Because of his poor grades, his father sent him to military school and he eventually served in the army. But unlike most leaders in history, Churchill did not rise to lead his people in battle with a sword or a gun. Instead, he inspired their courage and strength with words. His gift for the English language helped him lead the English people through the darkest days of their history.

Churchill was born prematurely on November 30, 1874, at Blenheim Palace in the county of Oxfordshire. Growing up, he was lonely and unhappy. His father, Lord Randolph Churchill, was a politician who had little time for his son. Churchill's mother, Jennie Jerome, was the daughter of a

*"Churchill's gift for the English language helped him lead the English people through the darkest days of their history."*

wealthy American who once owned the *New York Times* newspaper. She was more interested in being a part of English society than in caring for her son. The young Churchill was ultimately raised by a devoted nurse.

## Writings Capture Attention

After graduating from Sandhurst Royal Military Academy in 1895, Churchill was given the rank of second lieutenant in the army. Over the next few years, he served in India and in Egypt where he became known not as a fighter but as a writer. Many London newspapers published his articles about the battles, and he eventually turned those articles into two books: *The Story of the Malakand Field Force* (1898) and *The River War* (1899). He resigned from the army in 1899, but went back into battle the following year, covering the South African War as a war reporter. Acting more like a soldier than a journalist, he was captured while trying to defend an English armored train. Eventually, he made a daring escape from a prison camp. With a reward posted for his capture, he traveled through the South African countryside to safety. He returned to England a military hero, and in 1900 he ran successfully for a seat in the House of Commons, the governing body of Parliament (England's legislative assembly).

Initially, Churchill was a conservative, but he soon disagreed with many of his party's positions and switched his allegiance to the Liberal party. When the liberals came to power in the Commons a few years later, his political ability was recognized and he was appointed to higher and higher government offices. During this time, he reformed prisons, regulated hours and wages for workers, and established a social security system for the elderly. In 1908, while he had been campaigning in Scotland, he met and married Clementine Hozier.

Churchill served in government, including as secretary of state for war, until he was voted out of office in 1922. For the next two years he stayed out of politics, painting landscapes and beginning the writing of a four-volume account of World War I, *The World Crisis*. In 1924, back with the Conser-

*Churchhill and U.S. President Franklin D. Roosevelt discuss war strategy in 1943.*

vative party, he regained his seat in the House of Commons. He did not hold any high government offices in the 1930s and spent much time completing his writing projects.

During this time Churchill also kept on eye on the growing Nazi party in Germany (see **Adolf Hitler**) and constantly warned his countrymen about its threat to England. His fears were well founded. World War II began when Germany invaded Poland on September 1, 1939. Two days later, England declared war on Germany and Churchill was appointed first lord of the admiralty (head of the navy). The following May, when Germany raided Belgium and Holland, King George VI made him prime minister (leader of the government).

## Speeches Inspire Courage

For the next five years, Churchill supervised every aspect of England's war effort. He made great speeches before Parliament and over the radio, encouraging the English to have hope and remain determined against the Germans. Shortly after he was named prime minister, he told the people of England: "We shall fight on the beaches, we shall fight on the landing-grounds, we shall fight in the fields and in the streets, we shall fight in the hills; we shall never surrender."

However, Churchill did more than give speeches. Along with U.S. President Franklin D. Roosevelt (see **Franklin D. Roosevelt**), he planned many of the military battles against Germany. And despite his countrymen's wishes, he cooperated with the communist Russian government, led by Joseph Stalin. Regardless of political views, Churchill did what he believed was best to keep England from falling into German hands. Germany finally surrendered in May 1945 and World War II came to an end.

Churchill had led his nation through one of the most dangerous times in its history, but his Conservative party lost the majority of seats in the House of Commons in the 1945 election. Although he had been reelected, he had to resign as prime minister. For the next six years, he tried to convince Western leaders of the growing threat of the Soviet Union and of the spread of communism. In his free time, he continued painting and writing. Many of his paintings were exhibited at the Royal Academy of Arts in London. His six-volume *Second World War,* which he began writing in 1948, won him the Nobel Prize in Literature in 1953.

Churchill was named prime minister again when the Conservatives won a narrow victory in the 1951 election. Two years later, Queen Elizabeth II knighted him, and he became known as Sir Winston Churchill. In July 1953 he suffered a stroke, but continued serving another two years before he resigned the office of prime minister. His last decade was peaceful, and he painted, wrote, and bred race horses on his farm. On April 9, 1963, the U.S. Congress made him an honorary American citizen. When Churchill died on January 24, 1965, a splendid state funeral was held and the entire world paid tribute.

# Constantine I

*Christian Roman emperor*

*Born February 27, 285,*
*Naissus (modern Nis, Yugoslavia)*

*Died May 22, 337,*
*Nicomedia (modern Izmit, Turkey)*

Ancient Roman emperors often were soldiers who rose to be leaders of the Empire by defeating all other soldiers who wanted to lead. When they became emperors, however, they thought they did so because they were the children of their gods, which made them gods, too. But, this idea changed when Constantine took over. He became emperor, he believed, not because he was a god but because he had been chosen by God, the Christian God. He thought the power and the wisdom to rule came to him through this "divine right." For the next 1,400 years, European kings would claim their thrones by this same notion.

In 284, a year before Flavius Valerius Constantinus (Constantine) was born, the general Diocletian became emperor of Rome. When he took control, the Roman Empire had been in a state of chaos for almost 100 years. Its borders had been constantly attacked and crossed by its enemies. Leaders of provinces it controlled, like Zenobia of Palmyra (see **Zenobia**), rebelled against its rule. Even cities within the Empire

*"Constantine sought to unify the Roman Empire by spreading Christianity throughout it."*

suffered from famine and wide-spread disease. But under Diocletian's reign this stopped. He restored order to the Empire by ruling like an autocrat—a leader with unlimited power. Citizens of the Empire lost their freedom to laws he passed and their money to taxes he raised. People began to work not for themselves but for the emperor and the Empire.

Since Diocletian could not watch over all the borders of the Roman Empire, he appointed his trusted officer Maximian in 286 to be emperor of the western half of the Empire while he controlled the East. He also gave Maximian the surname *Augustus:* this title of honor was used by all emperors after the original Augustus (see **Augustus**). Thus began the crack that would eventually divide the Roman Empire into the West Roman Empire and the East Roman Empire (known as the Byzantine Empire by the Middle Ages).

In 293, when Constantine was eight, Diocletian established a system whereby the two emperors would each select a man to serve as an associate emperor. These subemperors were called "Caesars"—a title originally used by early emperors to honor Julius Caesar (see **Julius Caesar**). These Caesars would replace the emperors when the time came, and would then select new Caesars themselves. Constantine's father, Constantius, was made Caesar in the West. Constantine was then held hostage by Diocletian to ensure that Constantius would remain loyal to Diocletian and not try to become an emperor too soon.

Both Diocletian and Maximian gave up their rule in 305, and Constantius and Galerius (Caesar in the East) were made emperors. Constantine was allowed to return to his father, but the following year Constantius died. Constantine, who had been made Caesar by his father before his death, was declared emperor in the West by the Roman troops now under his command. He then asked Galerius to recognize him as Augustus, which would make him coequal with Galerius. Galerius refused. He accepted Constantine as Caesar only, giving the title of Augustus to his own son Severus. This set off a rebellion, and over the next six years, six men competed for the two emperorships. In the West, Constantine, Maximian, and his son Maxentius battled for rule. Constantine defeated Maximian in

309, then met his son in battle on October 28, 312. It proved to be a turning point for Christianity in the Roman Empire.

## Sees Glowing Cross in Night Sky

During his rule, Diocletian had begun the practice of persecuting Christians throughout the Roman Empire. Constantine, on the other hand, had always been compassionate toward Christians: he even ended this practice in Gaul (France), Spain, and Britain when he took over his father's rule in 306.

On the night before his battle with Maximian, Constantine's devotion to the Christian faith became stronger. He believed he saw in the dark sky a glowing cross with the words "By this sign you will conquer." He viewed this vision as a sign from God telling him he had been chosen to rule Rome. The next day he was victorious and became emperor of the entire West. The Eastern Empire, meanwhile, came under the rule of Valerius Licinianus Licinius after he defeated his final opponent the following year.

In 313 Constantine and Licinius began their joint rule by meeting at Milan in northern Italy and issuing the so-called Edict of Milan. This order officially ended Christian persecution in the Empire by legalizing Christian worship. A 10-year period of uneasy peace ended in 324 when Constantine declared war on Licinius and defeated him in battle. For the next 13 years, Constantine was sole ruler of the Roman Empire.

## Builds Gleaming, Walled City

Shortly after his victory, Constantine tried to strengthen not only old Rome but Christianity as well. He realized both of these goals when he decided to build a second capital from which to rule. The place he chose was the ancient Greek city of Byzantium on the Bosporus strait between the Black Sea and Sea of Marmara (site of modern Istanbul, Turkey). With an excellent harbor, this spot could be defended from land and sea. It was easily accessible to both the Asian and German frontiers as well. After almost four years of construction, the city was dedicated on May 11, 330, in the name of its founder: Constantinople.

Through the building of this gleaming, walled city, Constantine actively promoted Christianity. He established a new form of church building: the basilica. This long, rectangular type of building was used in ancient Rome as a public hall for business or legal matters. But Constantine adapted it as a spiritual place to easily house the growing number of worshippers. This style of architecture has since become the pattern for Christian churches in Western culture.

Constantine sought to unify the Roman Empire by spreading Christianity throughout it. He enlarged and rebuilt churches in all the eastern provinces. He also called for the unity of the church, aware of the divisions between Christians even then. In 325 he sponsored the Council of Nicaea, a conference of 220 bishops that developed the Nicene Creed (a set of fundamental beliefs held by the church). Although Constantine secured the future of Christianity, he failed to secure the unity of the Empire. Shortly before his death in 337, Constantine divided the Empire among his sons and nephews hoping they would share power and rule together. It was not to be. The crack began by Diocletian soon became a gap, and the Empire, save for only a few years, was never united again.

# Eleanor of Aquitaine

*Duchess of Aquitaine,*
*queen of France, queen of England*

*Born 1122,*
*Aquitaine, France*

*Died 1204,*
*Fontevrault-l'Abbaye, France*

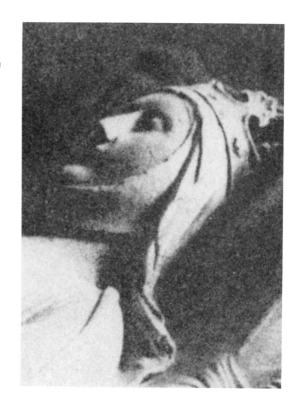

E leanor of Aquitaine held a tremendous amount of power in Western Europe during the Middle Ages. Over many years, her political reign spread from the region of Aquitaine to France to England. She wielded power not only through her own rule, but also through those of her children—two of her sons became kings of England. Her life, filled with political plots and ploys, even spawned literary legends that this beautiful and strong queen was possibly a murderer. Aside from her lasting part in medieval politics, Eleanor is best remembered for supporting the arts. Many artistic activities took place in her court, and Eleanor herself inspired the writing of many medieval love poems.

Eleanor was born in 1122 in Aquitaine, a powerful duchy (territory ruled by a duke) in southwest France. Her father was William X, duke of Aquitaine. Not much is known about her early childhood, although the influence of the arts on her life can be traced to her youth. Her father's court in Aquitaine was a center of learning and culture, and her grandfather William

*"Many artistic activities took place in her court, and Eleanor herself inspired the writing of many medieval love poems."*

IX was known as William the Troubadour. His poetry and music were widely admired throughout the south of France.

## Becomes Queen of France at 15

Eleanor's father died in 1137. Since she was the eldest child and had no brothers, she became duchess of Aquitaine and countess of Poitou (a region in west-central France that was part of the duchy of Aquitaine). This news was carried secretly and swiftly to the French king Louis VI. Hoping to strengthen his kingdom by linking with her powerful holdings, the king sent his son Louis VII to marry Eleanor. But before the young Louis and Eleanor had returned from their summer wedding, the old king was dead. At the age of 15, Eleanor was crowned queen of France.

Louis was not prepared to be king, however. His elder brother Philip was to be the heir, but died in a fall from a horse in 1131. Louis had been raised to enter the Church. He maintained many of the manners of a monk throughout his life, and this would eventually come between Louis and Eleanor. Another problem in their marriage was they could not produce an heir to the throne: Eleanor would eventually bear two daughters but no sons. The beginning of the end of their marriage came when Eleanor accompanied Louis in 1147 on the Second Crusade to Jerusalem in the Holy Land (see **Frederick I [Barbarossa]**). Against her wishes, Eleanor was forced to return with Louis after the crusade. Three years later, in 1152, she convinced the pope to dissolve her marriage to Louis, and within two months she married Henry, count of Anjou (a region in northwest France). This marriage soon proved more powerful than anyone could have imagined. Henry's mother was Matilda, the daughter of King Henry I of England. She and her son were rightful heirs to the English throne, but her cousin Stephen took control of it. Young Henry finally signed a treaty with Stephen that gave Henry the throne after Stephen's death. Stephen died in 1154, and Eleanor—duchess of Aquitaine, countess of Poitou and Anjou, became queen of England. As king of England, Henry II controlled more of France than Louis VII. This control is said to have caused the next 300 years of war between England and France.

# Artists Thrive in Her Court

In the first 13 years of their marriage, Eleanor bore Henry eight children. Five of them were sons: William, Henry, Richard, Geoffrey, and John. But King Henry was unfaithful, especially with a woman named Rosamond. Eleanor refused to tolerate his infidelities, and established her own court at Poitiers, the capital of Poitou. Here she created a great center for literary and musical activity. She spread the ideas of courtly love, a detailed system of rules that governed the way lovers should behave. These ideas—and life in Eleanor's court—are described in *The Art of Courtly Love,* written by Andreas Capellanus. It is considered one of the important books of the Middle Ages. The poet Chrétian de Troyes also wrote his great Arthurian romances at this time, including *Lancelot* and *Ywain.*

Eleanor's attention, however, was never far from politics. In 1169 Henry divided his kingdom among his sons, giving them titles but no real power. They rebelled in 1173 and Eleanor aided them. But Henry roundly defeated his sons on the battlefield and imprisoned Eleanor in Salisbury Castle shortly afterward. She remained there until 1185. (It was during this time that Henry's mistress, Rosamond, was killed. Later writers depict Eleanor as the murderer, but this most likely is not the case.)

When Henry died in 1189, Eleanor again became sole ruler over Aquitaine and Poitou. Only two of her sons were still alive: Richard and John. Richard, called "The Lionheart," claimed the English throne, and Eleanor returned to help her favorite son rule. Richard went on the Third Crusade in 1190, but was captured and held prisoner by the Holy Roman emperor. Before she secured his release, Eleanor ruled England, even stopping a rebellion by her son John.

Richard died suddenly in 1199, and John became king. Even though he was reportedly greedy, irresponsible, selfish, and cruel, he was Eleanor's son. So when her grandson Arthur claimed the throne that year, Eleanor helped John defeat him. She then aided John in his claims to Aquitaine, Anjou, and other French possessions. But his disloyalty and dishonesty cost him many other supporters, and he eventually lost most of the English holdings in France (only Aquitaine and a part of Poitou remained). By this time, Eleanor was in her eighties. She soon went to live among the nuns in the abbey of Fontevrault in western France, and died there in the spring of 1204.

# Elizabeth I

*English queen*

*Born September 7, 1533,
Greenwich Palace, England*

*Died March 24, 1603,
Richmond Palace, England*

Many historians agree that Elizabeth I was the most successful monarch ever to sit on the English throne. Her reign, known in English history as the Elizabethan Period, was an era of great accomplishment in England. It was a heroic age of exploration. Francis Drake sailed around the world, Martin Frobisher voyaged to the Arctic regions, and Walter Raleigh helped colonize America. Poets and dramatists like William Shakespeare and Edmund Spenser helped create the "Golden Age" of English literature. But it was Elizabeth herself who vastly changed England's standing among European nations. When she came to the throne England was a poor, remote island that was likely to become the next possession of the great Spanish Empire. By the time she died England had become a power in Europe, and its navy ruled the seas.

Elizabeth was born in 1533 in Greenwich Palace on the Thames River. Her father was the legendary king Henry VIII and her mother was Anne Boleyn, Henry's second wife. The

*"Despite the dark events of war and religious murders, Elizabeth's reign is best remembered for extraordinary achievements."*

## Humanism

The Renaissance (French for "rebirth") began in Italy in the late fourteenth century and spread through Europe by the seventeenth century. It was a period of great artistic achievement, with a rediscovery of the art and literature of the ancient Greeks and Romans. A philosophy that developed during this period was called Humanism. It opposed the medieval view that what mattered most in life was what happened to the soul after death. Humanists were more concerned with human values than spiritual ones. They turned away from the supernatural, focusing instead on the beauty and perfection they saw in the natural world and in the individual person. Humanists believed that through artistic and intellectual achievements a perfect life could be enjoyed in this world.

king (who eventually married six times) was obsessed with producing a son and heir. When Anne Boleyn couldn't give him one, he had her beheaded. Elizabeth, who was two years old at the time of her mother's death, was raised by four stepmothers. She received her education under the famous scholar and humanist Roger Ascham. Under his guidance, Elizabeth studied Greek and Roman classics, read history and theology, and learned both classical and modern languages. Extremely intelligent, she reportedly spoke six languages better than English during her youth.

Before her mother was executed, Elizabeth had been declared illegitimate. So when Henry VIII died in 1547, Elizabeth's half-brother became King Edward VI. But he died only six years later, and Elizabeth's half-sister Mary Tudor came to the throne. Mary, who was Catholic, earned the nickname "Bloody Mary" for burning many Protestants at the stake. When rebels wanted to place the Protestant Elizabeth on the throne, Mary had her arrested and sent to the Tower of London. She remained imprisoned for five years until Mary, near death, named Elizabeth her successor. On March 17, 1558, Elizabeth took the throne.

## Catholics Plot Against Elizabeth

Elizabeth initially did not want to face the heated conflict between Catholics and Protestants in England. But Mary, Queen of Scots (see **Mary, Queen of Scots**) forced her to do so. The Catholic Mary was the grandniece of Henry VIII and next in line to the throne. Accused of murdering her first husband, Henry Stewart Darnley, Mary fled to England to escape a rebellion in Scotland. Many European and English Catholics plotted to put her on the English throne. To protect her crown, Elizabeth had her cousin Mary placed under house arrest in 1567.

Meanwhile, Elizabeth's throne was threatened from outside forces. Philip II, who became ruler of Spain and its empire in 1556, sought to control the world. England and many other European countries were jealous of Spain's riches, especially in the New World. Elizabeth allowed her seamen to raid Spanish ships on the high seas. Between 1577 and 1580, Francis Drake sailed around the world, becoming the first man after Ferdinand Magellan to do so. On his trip, he ravaged Spanish settlements in South America, returning to England with £1,000,000 in treasure. Elizabeth knighted him aboard his ship, the Golden Hind, worsening already tense relations between Protestant England and Catholic Spain.

*Elizabeth signs the death warrant of Mary, Queen of Scots.*

During the 1580s, Elizabeth began to harshly persecute Catholics in England. She sent hundreds to their deaths. Many felt the horrors of the wrack, the manacles, and the Scavenger's Daughter. This last device was an iron hoop that brought a victim's hands, head, and feet together into a tight ball until he or she was crushed. Part of the reason for this persecution was a series of Catholic plots to murder Elizabeth and replace her with Mary, Queen of Scots. Finally, in 1586, Mary's part in these plots was proven. She was beheaded the following February.

## England Battles Spanish Armada

Mary's death was the final blow to English-Spanish relations. Philip II declared war. In July 1588, a huge navy fleet—the Spanish Armada—set sail for England. The English navy, led by Francis Drake and Martin Frobisher, rose to meet the armada in a nine-day battle. The smaller, quicker English ships easily outmaneuvered the Spanish galleons, but could not come close enough to attack. The Spaniards, however, made the mistake one night of anchoring their entire fleet, and the English sent a squadron of flaming ships into the anchored vessels. Frightened, the armada cut its lines and fled into open water. Chased by the English, the Spaniards tried to sail north around the British Isles. But storm after storm pounded the armada and nearly half the fleet was lost. The war continued for 15 years, but the Spaniards could not overcome the English. When Elizabeth died in 1603, Philip's dream of making England into a Catholic province ended.

Despite the dark events of war and religious murders, Elizabeth's reign is best remembered for extraordinary achievements. She believed it was her divine mission to lead England, and under her direction, the country became strong and unified. Commerce and industry prospered. The queen herself was an expert musician and her court was the cultural center of its day. Some of the great writers in English literature—Edmund Spenser, Philip Sidney, Christopher Marlowe, William Shakespeare—appeared during her reign. Spenser's masterpiece, *The Fairie Queen,* is even dedicated to her.

The Tudor family line of rulers, begun in 1485 with Henry VII, ended with Elizabeth's death. Her crown was taken by James I, son of Mary, Queen of Scots.

# Francis
# of Assisi

*Italian founder of Franciscan religious order*

*Born 1182,*
*Assisi, Italy*

*Died October 3, 1226,*
*Assisi, Italy*

He did not rule a kingdom, nor did he lead great armies into battle. Instead, Francis of Assisi led a divided—and, to some, strange—life. In his youth he lived in the carefree world of wealth. When he grew older, he gladly accepted the world of poverty and pain. He renounced, or gave up, everything he had: money, clothing, even family relations. All he wanted was to be a simple man, preaching the words of Jesus and the joys of living. Little did he know that he would lead a life that would serve as an inspiration, a model, for Catholics to this day.

Francis was born Giovanni (John) Bernardone to Pietro Bernardone, a cloth merchant, and his wife, Pica. Shortly after his birth, he was nicknamed "Francesco" ("Francis" in English) by his father. From his father he learned French, the language of international business, and he learned Latin, the main language of the Catholic Church. But he was never really interested in school, just barely learning how to read and to write. Later in life, he would sign his name with only a simple cross.

*"He heard the voice of Jesus say, 'Go, Francis, and repair my house, which is falling in ruins'"*

While he was growing up, Francis worked in his father's store. But what concerned Francis the most was his free time, which he spent with his friends. All of them were wealthy, and some of them were nobles, coming from royal or ruling families. Francis and his friends would spend their money on fine clothes and on evenings filled with eating, drinking, and singing. All Francis dreamed about then was becoming an honored soldier who would fight bravely in war and be knighted by his country's ruler. It was a dream shared by his father.

Not much else is known about Francis's early life. In 1201, when he was 19, the neighboring city of Perugia declared war on his hometown of Assisi. Francis was captured in battle the following November and held in a prison in Perugia for a year. Released in 1203, he returned home in poor health and stayed in bed for weeks. His illness changed him. After he was well, he no longer liked the games he and his friends used to play, nor the long evenings singing and drinking.

## Francis Dreams of God

Francis still wanted, however, to be a knight. So he went to help Pope Innocent III in his fight with German princes over who would rule the Holy Roman Empire. But Francis never made it to the Pope's army. While staying in the town of Spoleto, he dreamed that God spoke to him, telling him not to join the army but to return to Assisi. So he went back to his hometown.

Because his friends were off at war and the rest of the town thought he was a coward, Francis went to the churches around Assisi, praying for many hours by himself. In 1206, in the chapel of San Damiano, he heard the voice of Jesus say, "Go, Francis, and repair my house, which is falling in ruins." Francis thought God wanted him to repair churches stone by stone, so he began begging for money and building materials in the streets of Assisi.

Francis's clothes became dirty and ragged, and people laughed at him. In April 1207 his father saw him begging in front of his store. He took Francis to the authorities and then to the bishop, hoping they could convince his son to change his life. But in front of the bishop, Francis removed all of his clothes and announced, "I have called Pietro Bernardone my father ... now I will say Our Father who art in heaven."

Having left his family behind, Francis continued his task of rebuilding churches. In 1208, however, when he heard a reading from the Bible, he realized his mission should not be repairing broken stones and mortar, but restoring people's lives by telling them about the life of Jesus. He should live his life as Jesus had lived his, caring for the sick and depending on God for his own needs. Francis began preaching simply and joyously about Jesus' message and about all of God's creation, especially nature and animals.

## The Franciscan Order

The Franciscans are the largest religious order in the Roman Catholic church. Members of two of its branches live under strict vows of poverty and prayer. The Capuchins and the Poor Clares are among these members. A third branch is made up of lay people, individuals who combine everyday activity with teaching, charity, and social work. Famous members of this order include the Spanish explorer Christopher Columbus and the English philosopher and scientist Roger Bacon.

## Forms Religious Order

Francis's preaching reached many men. He went to Rome to meet with Pope Innocent III to ask permission to form a religious order, or group that lives according to a strict requirement or vow. At first the pope was unsure of the poorly clothed Francis. That night, however, the pope dreamed of a church beginning to fall to one side before it was held up by a small man dressed in rags. In the morning, the pope gave Francis his approval.

But men were not the only ones inspired by Francis. In 1212, a young noblewoman from Assisi, Clare, and her cousin, Pacifica, also wanted to follow Francis's way of life. After running away from home and seeking advice from Francis, they joined a convent. Soon, with others, they formed the Second Order of St. Francis, better known as the "Poor Clares."

But as the order of Franciscans grew, reaching outside Italy, Francis found it hard to preach about a simple life. His many duties prevented him from leading one. So late in his life, he prayed to suffer as Jesus had on the cross. Francis then received the stigmata (bleeding from the same wounds Jesus received on his hands, feet, and side when he was crucified).

These wounds stayed with Francis. He died shortly afterward at the age of 44, his body sickened by years of poverty and wandering. Two years later, in 1228, Francis was canonized, or declared to be a saint, by Pope Gregory IX.

# Frederick I (Barbarossa)

*King of Germany,*
*Holy Roman emperor, king of Italy*

*Born 1123*

*Died 1190,*
*Cilicia (in Asia Minor)*

After the reign of the Holy Roman emperor Otto (see **Otto I, the Great**), German kings struggled with the popes in Rome. The Holy Roman Empire stayed together, but only barely. Even the duchies (areas ruled by dukes) in Germany threatened to break away from one another. Then, in 1152, Frederick I came to the German throne and set out to regain the power of the monarchy. He managed to bring a sense of unity to a land that had been troubled by tribal differences for centuries. He added territory to the Holy Roman Empire, but he did not accomplish all he set out to do. Even so, Frederick—given the last name "Barbarossa," Italian for "Redbeard"—created a legend in his own lifetime. And the legend of a sleeping Barbarossa awakening to help a Germany in need lasts to this day.

Frederick was the son of Judith and Frederick, the duke of Swabia, a duchy located in the Black Forest in southwest Germany. His parents were members of two powerful rival families in Germany: the Hohenstaufen (father's side) con-

*"It is said that Frederick, his red beard still growing, will awaken when his country needs him and will lead it to victory."*

## The Crusades

The Holy Land is an area on the eastern shores of the Mediterranean Sea that includes the cities of Jerusalem, Nazareth, and Bethlehem. It was the birthplace of Jesus Christ (see **Jesus of Nazareth**) and Christianity. At the beginning of the Middle Ages, many Christians made trips—pilgrimages—to the Holy Land to see sacred shrines or monuments. In the seventh century, Arab Muslims raided and captured Jerusalem. They did not interfere with the pilgrims. But in the eleventh century, Seljuk Turks (also Muslims) conquered the Holy Land, and prevented Christians from going to the Holy Sepulchre, the church in Jerusalem built on the supposed site of Jesus' tomb. Between the eleventh and fourteenth centuries, European Christians, under a white flag with a red cross, led a series of nine Crusades (holy wars) to recover the Holy Land. They were all ultimately unsuccessful.

trolled Swabia while the Guelphs (mother's side) controlled the duchy of Bavaria. This connection to both families helped Frederick in his later rule. He became duke of Swabia in 1147 when his father retired to a monastery, and then accompanied his uncle, the Holy Roman emperor Conrad III, on the Second Crusade to Jerusalem in the Holy Land.

When Conrad III died in 1152, he designated Frederick as his heir. But this was just a "blessing," and Frederick had to be elected by the German nobility. Using cunning political measures, he was. Before he could be crowned Holy Roman emperor by the pope, however, he had to secure peace at home. He brought rebellious nobels under his control by granting them honors and by conferring with them on important political decisions. With his connections to the Hohenstaufen and Guelph families, Frederick was able to declare a general peace throughout the land. He also improved the feudal system (see **William the Conqueror**), bringing it more under his control. These combined actions strengthened his kingship in Germany.

Frederick also tried to improve his control over Italy. The Holy Roman Empire spread over this region, but previous emperors had neglected to maintain their power there. By the time Frederick sought the crown as Holy Roman emperor and king of Italy, the northern Italian provinces had almost complete control over themselves. Arnold of Brescia, a rebellious monk, had gained control of Rome, and in 1154 Frederick led his army into Rome (it was the first of six invasions he eventually led into Italy). He captured and hanged Arnold, and then was crowned emperor in 1155.

# Fights to Control Two Kingdoms

But Italians in the northern provinces, especially the Lombards, refused to bow to Frederick's will. So he was forced to return to Italy in 1158 to assert his authority in Lombardy. He was successful, capturing most of the cities and towns of this region. But over the next 20 years, Frederick had to shuttle between Italy and Germany to protect his power against uprisings. The greatest threat to Frederick's rule in Italy came from the Lombard League, a union of independent northern Italian cities. They organized in 1162 to resist his tax collectors and ruling officials. Frederick fought the Lombard League repeatedly until 1176, when he was soundly defeated at Legnano in northern Italy. Afterward, he made peace with the League.

Part of the reason Frederick lost at Legnano is that his troops were not supported by the German nobles, especially Henry the Lion, duke of Bavaria. While Frederick had been in Italy, Henry sought power outside of his duchy, destroying the unity Frederick brought to Germany. When Frederick returned from his defeat, he did not execute Henry. Instead, Frederick had Henry tried in court for breaking German law. Convicted in 1179, Henry was banished from the empire and his great land holdings were divided.

Over the next 10 years, Frederick reorganized his kingdom, trying to undo the damage Henry the Lion had done. In 1186 he arranged the marriage of his son and heir, Henry, to Princess Constance, heiress to the old Norman kingdoms of Sicily and southern Italy. Through this marriage, these lands were added to the empire. Frederick's work in his kingdom had not been completed when he decided to go with King Richard the Lion-Hearted of England and King Phillip II of France on the Third Crusade in 1189. This "Crusade of Kings," as it was called, proved to be a bad decision for Frederick. While crossing a river in Cilicia, an ancient country in southeast Asia Minor, he drowned. But soon the legend sprang up that the great Frederick Barbarossa was not dead. He was merely asleep, seated at a stone table in a cave in the German mountain Kyffhäuser. It is said that Frederick, his red beard still growing, will awaken when his country needs him and will lead it to victory.

# Frederick II, the Great

*King of Prussia*

*Born January 24, 1712,*
*Berlin, Prussia, present-day Germany*

*Died August 17, 1786,*
*Potsdam, Prussia*

*"Under Frederick's rule, Prussia became one of the great intellectual centers of Europe."*

In the eighteenth century, central Europe was divided into many so-called "German" states. The largest and strongest of these, Austria, was ruled by the powerful Habsburg family (see **Rudolf I**). When Frederick II came to power in 1740, his family, the Hohenzollerns, ruled over the separate and less powerful states of Brandenburg (located in present-day northeast Germany) and Prussia (present-day northeast Poland). By the time of his death 40 years later, Frederick had brought these states together and added territory, doubling the size of his kingdom. He increased its wealth, made it a great center of learning, and changed it into a military power stronger than Austria. For this, he became known to history as Frederick "the Great."

Frederick was born in 1712 in Berlin. His mother was Sophia Dorothea, daughter of King George I of England, and his father was Frederick William I, king of Prussia. The king oversaw young Frederick's education, making sure his tutors taught him only the basic skills of reading, writing, and mathematics. Secretly, his mother and his tutors taught Frederick music, literature, philosophy, and the arts. He thus became familiar with the philosophical movement known as the Enlightenment (see **Thomas Jefferson**). This movement emphasized the idea that there were basic laws behind life and that man's reason would help guide him to understand them. Among these laws were basic civil rights like freedom and the right to own property. It was the duty of governments, then, to protect these natural rights. This philosophy deeply influenced the thinking of the future king.

When Frederick's father found out about these secret teachings in 1728, he removed the tutors and placed his son under his complete control. Finally, in 1730, Frederick tried to escape from his hateful father to England, but he was captured and placed in prison. Before he was released a few months later, his father made him watch the beheading of his close friend who had helped plan his escape. The king then sent Frederick to rule over a few cities in Brandenburg and forced him to marry a German princess, Elizabeth Christina. Unfortunately, Frederick never loved her, and he eventually distanced himself from her. He would later die childless.

## Enlightened Ideas Guide Rule

Frederick became king of Prussia and elector of Brandenburg when his father died in 1740. Free to do as he wished, he tried to rule according to Enlightenment ideas. He reformed many laws and did away with the practice of torturing criminals. He gave food to the poor and had better roads and canals built. He also promoted education and allowed people to practice their own religion.

Above all, Frederick sought to make Prussia a great European power. In 1713 the Austrian king and Holy Roman emperor Charles VI had issued the Pragmatic Sanction. It called for Charles's daughter, Maria Theresa, to rule the Habsburg lands after him since he had no sons. All other European powers had to agree to this sanction. Frederick's father agreed only after Charles promised to give him two small German provinces in return. But Charles soon withdrew his promise.

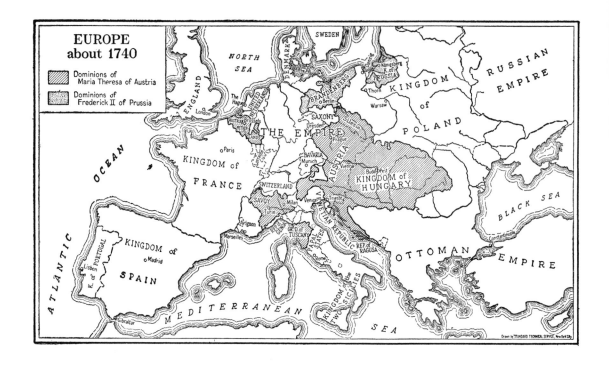

EUROPE
about 1740

Dominions of
Maria Theresa of Austria

Dominions of
Frederick II of Prussia

When Maria Theresa came to the throne in 1740, Frederick sought revenge for his father.

Southwest of Prussia lay the territory of Silesia, a rich industrial and farm province, double the size and population of Brandenburg-Prussia. Since it could make his kingdom powerful and since it belonged to Austria, Frederick seized it in 1740, starting the First Silesian War. The Austrians nearly defeated the Prussians at first, but the tide turned. Prussia was then joined by France, a long-time enemy of the Habsburgs. Wanting to protect her other territories against the more dangerous French, Maria Theresa agreed to end her battle with Frederick. In 1742 they signed the Treaty of Breslau, which gave Silesia to Prussia. Frederick pulled out of the war, leaving France to fight alone.

Maria Theresa soon began to defeat the French with the help of England, France's colonial rival in America. Frederick feared that if France lost, England and Austria would unite against Prussia. So in 1744 he tore up the Treaty of Breslau and personally led an attack against Austria. In this Second

Silesian War Frederick won a series of brilliant victories and a reputation as a military genius. Just one year later, England pulled out of the war and Maria Theresa was forced to sign another treaty with Frederick. The Treaty of Dresden in 1745 again recognized Prussia's control of Silesia.

## Creates Cultural Center

That same year Frederick began a decade of peace in Prussia by building a royal palace in the city of Potsdam, outside of Berlin. Surrounded by orange groves and cherry orchards, the magnificent palace of Sans Souci (French for "without care") was over 300 feet long and housed a great library. Here Frederick wrote poetry and studies on history and politics. He learned to play the flute and composed sonatas and concertos (many are still performed in concerts). To Sans Souci, Frederick brought ballet and opera companies from around Europe. And he entertained many philosophers, musicians, and artists, including the French writer François Voltaire. Under his rule, Prussia became one of the great intellectual centers of Europe.

Peace in Prussia ended in 1756 when Frederick made two costly mistakes. Fearing an attack by Russia, Frederick signed a treaty of protection with England. But this angered the French—they felt Frederick had abandoned them a second time. So when Maria Theresa, who still wanted Silesia back, asked France to help her if Prussia attacked, the French agreed. The allies were now switched: it was Prussia and England against Austria and France.

Frederick's second error was thinking Russia might join with Austria and France. To prevent this he invaded the Austrian-controlled state of Saxony to the south of Brandenburg in 1756. He planned on returning it only if Maria Theresa did not join in an alliance with Russia. His plan backfired. France declared war on Prussia, and the Seven Years' War began. The following year Russia did indeed join with Austria and France against Prussia and England. Since England was fighting France in America, however, Frederick had to fight Austria and Russia in Europe by himself. He received a stroke of luck when an admirer of his, Peter III, took over Russia in 1762 and pulled it out of the war. Without Russian help, Maria Theresa was forced to sign the Peace of Hubertusburg in 1763, giving permanent control of Silesia to Prussia.

Frederick added further territory to his kingdom in 1772. He convinced the Russian empress Catherine II (see **Catherine II, the Great**) to divide up Poland, over which she had control. The land Frederick received joined Prussia to Brandenburg, and for the first time, the Hohenzollern lands were connected. Frederick spent the remainder of his life focusing on the arts and Prussia continued to be a cultural center. He died at Sans Souci on August 17, 1786, his throne taken over by his nephew, Frederick William II.

# Mikhail Gorbachev

*Leader of Union of
Soviet Socialist Republics (U.S.S.R)*

*Born March 2, 1931,
Privolnoe, U.S.S.R. (now Russia)*

For almost 70 years the Communist party ran the government of the Union of Soviet Socialist Republics, more commonly known as the Soviet Union. The Communists tightly controlled almost all aspects of life in the country, and anyone who disagreed with them was severely punished. This all changed, though, when Mikhail Gorbachev became leader of the Soviet Communist Party. He introduced economic and social reforms that radically transformed the lives of the Soviet people and had a profound effect on nations around the world. The political relationship between the Soviet Union and the United States was improved and the threat of global nuclear war was reduced. But Gorbachev did not foresee that his countrymen, controlled for so long, would rise up with their new freedoms to put an end to his leadership and to the Soviet Union.

Gorbachev was born in 1931 to Maria Panteleyevna Gorbacheva and Andreyevich Gorbachev, an agricultural engineer. He was raised in the tiny farm village of Privolnoe near the Caucasus Mountains in the southwestern region of the

*"Gorbachev introduced economic and social reforms that radically transformed the lives of the Soviet people and had a profound effect on nations around the world."*

## Stalin: "Man of Steel"

Joseph Stalin (1897-1953) was a strict dictator who was feared by many, both inside and outside the Soviet Union. While growing up he studied to be a priest. He was expelled when he became involved with Marxism and the Bolshevik Party. Before the Russian Revolution in 1917, he changed his name from Dzhugashvili to Stalin, which means "man of steel." After Vladimir Lenin died in 1924, Stalin took control of the Soviet Union. Within five years he began his collective farms program. When the peasant farmers resisted, they were sent to labor camps or killed. Although millions perished, Stalin was not satisfied. In 1934 he began a series of "purge" trials, accusing many old Bolsheviks of trying to overthrow the government. Thousands were convicted and sent to prison or executed. Soon, there was no one left to challenge his authority.

Soviet Union. Only two years before he was born, the Communist dictator Joseph Stalin had ordered all private farms and animals seized and placed under government control. Peasant farmers were forced to work on what were now called collective farms. The government dictated what would be grown, how much of it, and what the farmers would be paid for their work. Many members of Gorbachev's family were peasant farmers and he, too, worked on the collective farms while growing up.

In 1950 Gorbachev entered Moscow State University, the most distinguished university in the Soviet Union. He studied law, but took courses in many fields and received a broad education. While in school he met and married a philosophy student, Raisa Maksimovna Titorenko. He also joined the Communist Party, and after graduating in 1955 he went to the city of Stavropol near his hometown to work for the party. He rose through the leadership ranks during the next fifteen years to become the party leader in Stavropol in 1970. At the same time he was elected to the Supreme Soviet, the highest legislative body in the Soviet Union.

Yuri Andropov, head of the KGB (secret police), was from Stavropol and took Gorbachev under his wing. Perhaps with Andropov's influence, Gorbachev was named the agricultural secretary of the Communist Party in 1978. Just two years later, he joined the Politburo, the ruling body of the party. His high standing among the Communists at this time was unusual because of his age. While most leaders were in their seventies, Gorbachev was under fifty.

Andropov became general secretary (leader) of the party in 1982 following the death of Leonid Brezhnev. As Andropov's key assistant, Gorbachev took control of the running of the economy. When Andropov died two years later, Konstantin Chernenko was chosen instead of Gorbachev to become the new leader. But when Chernenko died in early 1985, Gorbachev was finally appointed general secretary of the Communist Party, making him the effective leader of his country.

## *Perestroika* and *Glasnost*

Gorbachev immediately began a campaign of reforms in the Soviet Union. He forced many conservative Communist leaders out of government and replaced them with younger members who shared his views. He began policies called *perestroika* ("restructuring") and *glasnost* ("openness") that removed government controls over the economy and allowed the Soviet people to openly discuss the problems facing their country. When the nuclear reactor at Chernobyl exploded on April 26, 1986, the Soviet government initially tried to cover up the incident. But Gorbachev, remaining true to *glasnost,* felt it was important to tell the entire world of the disaster.

Gorbachev also sought peace abroad and at home. After a series of summit conferences, he and United States President Ronald Reagan signed a treaty in 1987 limiting the number of nuclear weapons each country could have. Gorbachev decided to end the Afghanistan War begun in 1978, which pitted anti-Communist Afghans against their government and the Soviet Union. By 1989 all Soviet troops were removed from that country. For all of his peace efforts, Gorbachev was awarded the Nobel Peace Prize in 1990.

Gorbachev's most important change in the Soviet Union came in 1989 when he allowed other political parties to run against the Communists in general elections. This was a significant decision as the Communists had controlled the Soviet Union since the Russian Revolution in 1917. The Communists lost their power and Gorbachev separated himself from them by taking the position of Soviet President. The Communist dictatorship had ended.

## Berlin Wall Comes Down

With the weakening of communism in Eastern Europe, many countries and ethnic groups wanted their independence.

In 1989 the Berlin Wall came down, and East and West Germany were reunited. In 1990 Lithuania became the first of the Baltic states to declared its independence from the Soviet Union. And in the Soviet-controlled republics of Armenia and Georgia, ethnic wars broke out. Gorbachev sought to maintain some control over these areas, but his own position at home was in trouble. His plan to gradually release government control of farms and industry wasn't happening fast enough for the Soviet people. Because they had suffered in poverty for many years, they wanted quicker reforms. A chief critic of Gorbachev was Boris Yeltsin, who had been elected president of the Russian Republic in June 1991.

On the other hand, conservative members of the Politburo thought Gorbachev was giving away too much power. In August 1991 they kidnapped him in hopes of regaining control of the government. But this August Coup (overthrow of the government) failed after only four days when Yeltsin rallied the Russian people against the Communist leaders. Gorbachev returned to Moscow, though Yeltsin now had the support of the majority of people. Gorbachev then dissolved the Communist Party, admitting later that the defeat of communism was "a victory for common sense, reason, democracy, and common human values."

Gorbachev granted independence to the remaining republics that had been controlled by the Soviet Union. On December 8, 1991, a new economic federation—the Commonwealth of Independent States—was formed among those republics. The government of the Soviet Union could no longer function. On Christmas Day Gorbachev resigned the office of president, becoming a private citizen. At midnight on December 31, 1991, the red Communist flag with its gold hammer and sickle was lowered in Moscow and the Union of Soviet Socialist Republics came to an end.

# Gregory I, the Great

*Pope of Catholic Church*

*Born c. 540,*
*Rome, present-day Italy*

*Died 604,*
*Rome*

The Catholic Church had grown in the Roman Empire since the time of Constantine I (see **Constantine I**). But when the Western Empire fell in 476, the Church's existence in Rome was threatened. The half-ruined city was open to attacks, fever, famine, and plagues (wide-spread diseases). For protection, the Church was reliant now on the Eastern Empire (Byzantine Empire), based in Constantinople. The Church may not have survived had it not been for Gregory I. During his 14-year reign as pope (bishop of Rome), he made the Church less dependent on the Empire by negotiating with the enemies of Rome himself. He better organized the internal life of the Church: He called for stricter discipline among churchmen, and established a liturgy (mass) for Catholics everywhere. He even helped develop one of the timeless musical forms of Catholic worship, the Gregorian chant.

Born in about 540, Gregory came from a rich and powerful Roman family. Although Rome had already been invaded and sacked by the Goths (a Germanic tribe), a Roman society

*"Gregory laid the basis for the Church to operate independently and for the office of the pope truly to direct the governing of it throughout the world."*

still existed. Having received a classical education, Gregory rose quickly through the ranks of governing officials of the city. He finally reached the position of prefect of Rome (the city's highest office) by 573. But just a few years later, he resigned this position. Always a devout Catholic, he decided to become an ordinary monk and turned his seven houses into Benedictine monasteries.

Gregory lived as a monk for six years before Pope Gelasius II asked him to become a papal legate (ambassador of the church) to the emperor's court in Constantinople. There Gregory gained a reputation for being a tough-minded and practical administrator. He also was noted for his strict lifestyle: he often fasted and inflicted pain on himself as a way to remain true to his spiritual calling. But this ruined his health for the rest of his life. When Pope Gelasius II died in 590 and Gregory was elected the new pope, he did not accept the position at first—he was too sick.

## Becomes Pope Who Serves

But Gregory soon decided it was his duty to become pope. Weak and growing with pain, he took on the tasks of his new throne. He continued to live his harsh life, though, emphasizing his role was to serve, rather than to command. He became the first to take the title—used by popes ever since—"Servant of the Servants of God."

When Gregory became pope, the western world was undergoing great changes. Old Rome was fading and fierce tribes were establishing kingdoms throughout Europe. The Lombards, a Germanic people who set up a kingdom in northern Italy in 568, began reaching down into central Italy and into Rome. The seemingly unending war and constant plagues led many Christians to believe the Apocalypse, or end of the world, was near. Gregory, who was very superstitious, also believed the Apocalypse was extremely close. He felt it was his task to bring as many people as possible into the Christian faith before the catastrophe struck.

This belief led Gregory to try to restore order to the area around Rome. He had the Church take over the civic duties previously run by the Empire. These included judging court cases and distributing free grain to the people during times of famine. He was not above using the sword to defend the Church and the Italian people either. Gregory paid soldiers— and arranged for monks—to help defend Rome against opposing armies. And he used Church funds to ransom prisoners, even selling Church treasures in order to raise the money.

At the same time, Gregory strengthened the internal order of the Church. He disciplined those bishops who bought and sold the offices they held and those who lived with women rather than obeying the law of celibacy. Indeed, Gregory sought to cleanse the Church of all practices by its members that differed from original Church customs and teachings. Many leaders in the Church thought Gregory was too harsh in his approach, but he believed the Church would be stronger if it were pure.

## Negotiates With Enemies of Rome

Gregory soon realized the Church could not achieve its full strength without befriending its enemies. Ignoring the Roman Empire, which did not help him anyway, he negotiated a treaty with the Lombards. Gregory arranged a general halt in the fighting (although isolated attacks continued throughout his reign and even after his death) and laid the foundation for the Lombards' conversion to Christianity. He also came to terms with the Franks and the Visigoths, tribes in the territories that make up modern France and Spain.

Perhaps the greatest act of Gregory's reign as pope was his conversion of the Anglo-Saxon tribes in England. He sent Augustine, the head monk of his Roman monastery, to carry out this mission. But as with the other peoples of Europe, converting the Anglo-Saxons to Christianity was a slow task. Often, people in these tribes just added Christian practices to their other religious rituals. Nonetheless, the mission was successful: Christianity gained a foothold in this region, and it grew in the centuries to come.

With these contacts—Lombards, Franks, Visigoths, Anglo-Saxons—Gregory gave the Church the chance to act outside territory that was politically friendly. His work brought about the idea of "Christendom," or a Christian kingdom. Though the kingdoms of Europe might be split apart politically, they would be united in the Catholic faith. Thus, Gregory laid the basis for the Church to operate independently and for the office of the pope truly to direct the governing of it throughout the world. Because of many miracles supposedly connected to Gregory during his life and even following his death, the Church declared him a saint.

# Gustavus Adolphus

*Swedish king*

*Born December 9, 1594,
Stockholm, Sweden*

*Died November 16, 1632,
Lützen, Germany*

Most people would not think that war had a place in Sweden's history, since this country has not been at war since 1814 (it remained neutral in both World War I and II). In almost every year since 1901, the Swedish government has handed out Nobel Prizes for achievements in literature, in the sciences, and, especially, in world peace. This nonviolent image of Sweden, however, has not always existed. During the seventeenth century it controlled an empire that stretched over Finland, the south shore of the Baltic Sea, and areas in northern Germany. Sweden's kings obtained this empire mainly through battle; its greatest soldier king was Gustavus Adolphus.

Born in Stockholm in 1594, Gustavus was the eldest son of Charles IX and his wife, Christina. Under his father's supervision, the intelligent Gustavus studied Greek and Roman literature, mathematics, law, history, and eight languages, speaking German fluently. As future leader of the Swedish army, he received a thorough military education, training under Swe-

*"Gustavus's great achievements earned him a place in Swedish history as the 'father of the fatherland.'"*

den's best general. But his young life was not always filled with serious studies. He loved music and dancing, and he took part in these activities throughout his life.

In 1611, when he was not yet 17, Gustavus succeeded his father to the Swedish throne. Almost immediately he set about reforming the government. Throughout history, nations were often torn between kings and nobles over the fight for control. This had been the case in Sweden. When Gustavus came to power, however, he sought to work with the nobility, not to fight with them. Under the Charter of 1611, he granted the control of certain government offices to the nobility. And he chose Axel Oxenstierna, a high-ranking noble, to be his chancellor and administrator. Their close relationship helped stabilize the kingdom. Gustavus established Sweden's first independent supreme court, an advanced system of high schools, better government administration, and tax collection. Before Gustavus, Sweden did not have a central government. By 1626, after he had ruled for 15 years, Sweden had the most efficient government in Europe.

## Begins Building Empire

Gustavus began these reforms in part to strengthen Sweden against its enemies. In 1611 Denmark had invaded Sweden, trying to restore the union of Scandinavian countries brought about in the late fourteenth century by Margaret I of Denmark (see **Margaret I**). Gustavus ended this war in 1613, but he had to pay the Danes to keep Sweden free. Meanwhile, Poland had been trying to gain territory in Russia since 1600, and Sweden had been trying to block it. In 1617 Gustavus was able to take Ingermanland, a historic region in Russia along the east bank of the Gulf of Finland, thus ending Poland's eastward drive. To secure his position in northern Germany, he married Maria Eleonora, daughter of George William, Elector of Brandenburg.

Gustavus still did not feel safe, so he invaded Livonia (modern Estonia and Latvia) in 1620. Within six years the country was under his control, and he then moved against Polish ports along the Baltic Sea. By 1630 Gustavus had signed two treaties with Poland giving him this land.

Gustavus's last objective was to keep Sweden out of the Thirty Years' War. Begun in 1618, this war pitted Protestant German nobles against the Catholic Holy Roman emperor Ferdinand II. In addition to religious reasons, the nobles fought the emperor to prevent him from gaining more power in the Holy Roman Empire. The war soon spread throughout the Baltic Sea region as countries chose religious sides. Feeling his control over the Baltic threatened, Gustavus was forced to take part. In 1630 he took his army to Germany on behalf of the Protestants.

Through his study of current military techniques, Gustavus made the Swedish army the best fighting force in the world at that time. It was a national army that men joined freely. Highly trained and disciplined, the soldiers responded well to the king's motivating leadership.

## Military Tactics Lead to Victory

The Swedish army swept across the northern German soil. In September 1631 Gustavus met count Johannes Tilly, leader of the emperor's forces, at the city of Breitenfeld in northern Germany. Even though the Swedish army was badly outnumbered, it was technically superior. Instead of charging their enemies with pikes (wooden poles with pointed metal heads), the Swedes shot them with muskets. Additionally, they moved rapidly in small groups, easily crushing the large and disorganized army of the emperor. This victory saved Protestantism in Germany and gave Gustavus control over the northern part of the country. This battle not only changed the balance in the Thirty Years' War but the way war has been fought ever since.

After spending the winter in northern Germany, Gustavus decided in April 1632 to move his army south. Crossing the Lech River north of the city of Augsburg, he met Tilly again. This time the count was killed in battle, which left all of Bavaria (the southern part of Germany) open to Gustavus. At the same time he was forced to return north to save cities threatened by the emperor's army, now led by general Albrecht von Wallenstein. In November 1632 the two commanders met at Lützen, outside the city of Leipzig.

During his military career, Gustavus was almost killed many times. One horse had been shot from under him; two others had fallen through ice beneath him. From an earlier battle, Gustavus carried an unoperable musket ball inside his neck. But his luck ran out at Lützen. Just as the battle was beginning, Gustavus was shot and his horse bolted to the other side. His body, stripped by looters, ended up face down in the mud.

Oxentierna then directed the country until Gustavus's young daughter Christina became old enough to rule in 1644. The war finally ended 16 years after Gustavus's death when the remaining leaders signed the Peace of Westphalia in 1648, reducing the power of the Holy Roman emperor. Sweden came out of the Thirty Years' War a victor. Gustavus had left his country with an excellent army, an efficient government, and a stable society. Although his Baltic empire lasted only 100 years, his great achievements earned him a place in Swedish history as the "father of the fatherland."

# Adolf Hitler

*Leader of Nazi Germany*

*Born April 20, 1889,
Braunau, Upper Austria*

*Died April 30, 1945,
Berlin, Germany*

When Adolf Hitler was a teenager, he saw a performance of the opera *Rienza* by the famous German composer Richard Wagner. In the opera the hero frees his people from the cruel and humiliating rule of their enemy. At this time, Hitler thought he would grow up to become an artist, and the music of *Rienza* moved him. But he was touched deeper by its story, which strengthened his growing desire to "save" German culture. He believed Germans were to be the masters of the world, and he would do whatever it took to make it so. Hitler dreamed of making a Third *Reich* ("state") in Germany that would last for a thousand years. It would surpass the ancient German glories of the Holy Roman Empire and the kingdom of Frederick I (see **Frederick I [Barbarossa]**). His dream, however, eventually ended in 1945. His "Thousand-Year *Reich*" lasted only 12 years—and left more than 50 million dead.

Hitler, the son of Alois and Klara Hitler, was born in 1889 in a small town in Austria. His father was an official with

*"Hitler believed Germans were to be the masters of the world, and he would do whatever it took to make it so."*

the Austrian Customs Service and was able to provide his family with a comfortable living. The young Hitler was intellectually above average, but did well only in those school subjects that interested him. Most of the time he was bored in school. So he dropped out when he turned 16, two years after his father's death.

## A Strong Sense of Nationalism

When Hitler's mother died in 1907, he then moved to Vienna to enter the Academy of Fine Arts with hopes of becoming a painter. He did not have enough artistic talent, however, and the Academy twice denied him admission. He ended up living on the streets, selling postcards he painted of Viennese landmarks. Beyond his lack of talent, Hitler's mind at this time was closed to any new ideas. It was filled only with the hateful ideas of prejudice. Because of the long rule of the Habsburg family (see **Rudolf I**), German culture extended over Austria. Hitler had grown up believing that this culture was superior to all others (a belief called "nationalism") and that it had to be defended against them. The greatest threat to Germany and to its culture, he believed, came from Jewish people, whom he blamed for social uprisings and economic problems.

After moving to Munich, Germany, in 1913, Hitler was called back to Austria to take a physical for the army, but he was declared medically unfit to serve. He volunteered for the German army and was accepted when World War I broke out in 1914. He spent the entire four years of the war at the front lines, and he earned the Distinguished Iron Cross for bravery. He later said that serving as a soldier in battle was "the greatest and most unforgettable time" of his life. When World War I ended in 1918 and Germany was forced to sign the strict Treaty of Versailles (which strongly limited Germany's power), Hitler cried. It was the first time he had done so since his mother's death 11 years earlier. He convinced himself that Germany had not lost on the battlefield, but had been brought down by "un-German" forces (Jews, liberals, socialists). He pledged to return Germany to a position of power and respect.

After the war, Hitler's military leaders ordered him to spy on a political organization in Munich called the German Workers' Party. Sharing the party's ideals of extreme nationalism, he eventually joined them. In 1920 the group renamed itself the National Socialist German Workers' Party, or the Nazi Party for short. Pushing aside all rivals, Hitler became leader of the arty in 1921. Within two short years, he made the Nazis into a military-like organization and ruled them like a dictator—his word was law.

## First Attempt at Power

In November 1923 Hitler tried to seize power in Germany. In a beer hall outside of Munich, important government officials were speaking to a large gathering of men. Suddenly, Hitler and his Nazi militia (called stormtroopers) burst in and tried to force the officials to declare a revolution. This *putsch* ("attempt to seize power") failed when the officials escaped. The following day, Hitler and his stormtroopers marched on the War Ministry building and were fired on by police. Hitler escaped, only to be found a few days later and arrested for high treason. Instead of life imprisonment, though, Hitler was given a sentence of five years of comfortable confinement (not hard labor). He eventually served only nine months.

While jailed in a fortress in Landsberg, Hitler dictated his autobiography, *Mein Kampf* ("My Struggle"). Although poorly written, the book clearly outlined Hitler's ideas about the world and the direction he wanted Germany to take. He stated that Germans (what he called the "Aryan" race) were the highest "creators of culture" in the world and should be the masters of it. All other races were to serve them. But some races, especially the Jews, were "destroyers of culture" and were unfit to even serve. They had to be destroyed.

After Hitler was released in 1925, he tried to have the Nazis elected to public office. But people did not listen to him until the world economic situation worsened after the 1929 New York stock market crash. Many Germans, now jobless, began to hear Hitler's powerful message of a Third *Reich*. He was a g:fted public speaker, and he played on the unemployed

German's fears. In 1930 the Nazis won enough votes to make them the second-most powerful political party in Germany. President Paul von Hindenburg then named Hitler chancellor (head minister) of Germany in January 1933.

## Nazis Gain Power

Hitler and the Nazis moved quickly and brutally to seize power. On February 27 a fire destroyed part of the building of the *Reichstag* (the German parliament). Although the fire was started by one man who was a communist, Hitler used this as an excuse to begin a reign of terror against all other political enemies. It worked: The parliament granted the Nazis "legal" powers allowing them to take over the country. The Nazis soon created concentration camps to punish political enemies. On May 10 they burned huge piles of books they considered "un-German"—books by such writers as Jack London, H.G. Wells, Helen Keller, and Albert Einstein. All other political parties were outlawed; only the Nazis existed. As *Fürher* ("leader"), Hitler had become an unchallenged dictator.

Hitler set out to achieve the goals he outlined in *Mein Kampf*. He took Germany out of the League of Nations (an association of nations formed to settle world conflicts) and began re-arming the German military, a violation of the Treaty of Versailles. In 1935 he passed the so-called Nuremberg Laws, which took away the civil rights of Jews in Germany and forbid marriages between Germans and Jews. To make sure no one questioned or broke Nazi laws, Hitler created a secret police force, the *Geheime Staatspolizei*, better known as the Gestapo. Anyone who objected to the Gestapo was almost certainly tortured and killed.

Hitler began building his German empire in 1938 by taking control of Austria and of German-speaking regions of Czechoslovakia. Since a single shot had not been fired in the takeover, the rest of Europe stood by. But when his military invaded Poland on September 1, 1939, Europe decided to act. Two days later, England and France declared war and World War II was underway. The first years of the war went well for Hitler. By the middle of 1940, he had captured France and controlled most of Europe. He turned his attention to Russia in 1941, hoping to destroy it quickly. But the Russian people fiercely resisted the German assaults.

America entered the war at the end of 1941, and Hitler became reckless. Sensing that victory might slip away from him, he ordered what he called the "Final Solution to the Jewish Question"—the mass killing of European Jews in German concentration camps. Hitler's dream was fading, though, and those around him soon realized it. On July 20, 1944, some of his military leaders tried to assassinate him, but the attempt failed. Hitler took vicious revenge, killing about 5,000 people he believed were involved in the plot.

Hitler knew the end was near. Beginning in January 1945 he never left his underground bunker in Berlin. As the Russian army closed in on the city, Hitler refused to flee. On April 29, he married Eva Braun, his long-time mistress. He then dictated his will, in which he blamed everyone but himself for the troubles that had plagued the world since 1933. The following day, Eva drank poison and Hitler shot himself. By his orders, their bodies were taken to an outside garden and burned.

# Isabella I

*Spanish queen of Castile*

*Born April 22, 1451,
Madrigal de las Altas Torres, Castile*

*Died November 26, 1504,
Medina del Campo, Spain*

# Ferdinand II

*Spanish king of Aragon*

*Born March 10, 1452,
Sos, Aragon*

*Died January 23, 1516,
Madrigalejo, Spain*

Known as the Catholic Monarchs, Isabella I and Ferdinand II are among the most important rulers in Spanish history. Ruling jointly, they brought together the Spanish kingdoms on the Iberian Peninsula—the geographical territory in southwest Europe where Spain and Portugal now sit. The unified kingdom they formed helped lead to the creation of the modern country of Spain.

Through marriage alliances, conquests in Europe, and explorations and conquests in the Americas, Ferdinand and Isabella began the formation of a Spanish Empire. Their determination to spread Catholicism throughout Spain, however, resulted in a system that killed many people and forced many others to flee the country. This harsh system is known to history as the Spanish Inquisition.

When Isabella and Ferdinand were born in the middle of the fifteenth century, Spain was divided into five main kingdoms: Castile (north-central), Aragon (east), Portugal (west), Navarre (far north), and Granada (south). Governments and

> "The unified kingdom Isabella and Ferdinand formed helped lead to the creation of the modern country of Spain."

even languages differed in each one. To complicate matters, Castile and Aragon, the largest kingdoms, were made up of several provinces with further language differences.

Ferdinand was born in 1452 to King John (Juan) II of Aragon and Juana Enríquez of Castile. His education focused on the martial arts, but as a Renaissance prince he also studied Latin, history, and music. Although he was not immediately in line to receive his father's kingship, he did become heir to the throne when his elder brother died in 1461. In 1468, when he was 15 years old, his father made him king of Sicily, the Mediterranean island off the coast of Italy that Aragon controlled then.

Isabella was born in 1451 to King John (Juan) II of Castile and Isabella of Portugal. She, also, was not expected to rule. She was raised to follow what was then considered the womanly role of wife, mother, and devout Christian. Her father died in 1454 and her half-brother became king as Henry IV. But when Isabella's younger brother died and Henry IV's only child was thought to be illegitimate, Henry had to recognize her as his heir.

Isabella and Ferdinand were married in October of 1469. Although this union between Castile and Aragon seemed logical, many people in both kingdoms were opposed. In 1470 Henry IV declared that his daughter, Juana, was legitimate and, therefore, was his rightful heir. But Isabella convinced the Castilian nobility to support her, and when Henry died in 1474 she was proclaimed queen of Castile.

## Become Rulers of Castile and Aragon

The strongest threat to Isabella and Ferdinand's rule in Castile came when King Alfonso of Portugal became engaged to Juana and pressed for her right to the throne. Beginning in 1476 Ferdinand led a series of attacks against the invading Portuguese army. By 1479 he defeated Portugal and took claim to Castile. Isabella was recognized as its proper ruler. That same year Ferdinand's father died, and he became ruler of Aragon, Sicily, and Sardinia, another Mediterranean island controlled by Aragon.

Although Isabella and Ferdinand co-ruled both Castile and Aragon, they allowed the separate customs and identities of the two kingdoms to continue. Isabella made the final decisions in Castile while Ferdinand made those in Aragon. The way they jointly signed important documents and the way they advised each other on political matters reflected their deep desire to unify Spain.

*Isabella and Ferdinand with Christopher Columbus*

In 1479 Isabella and Ferdinand set out to recapture the Moorish kingdom of Granada. In the eighth century, Arab Muslims from the northern coast of Africa invaded and captured most of Spain. Throughout the Middle Ages, Spaniards tried to reconquer (*reconquista*) these lands from the Muslims, who were known to the Spanish as Moors. By the fifteenth century, the Moors only occupied Granada in the south. For over a decade, Ferdinand and his forces fought for the control of this kingdom. Finally, in 1492 Granada surrendered, completing the *reconquista*.

## Establish the Spanish Inquisition

Another reason Isabella and Ferdinand drove the Moors from Spain was because they were Muslims, not Catholics. After the Moors left, several religions—including Islam and Judaism—still existed in Spain beside Catholicism. To further rid their kingdom of non-Christians, Isabella and Ferdinand established a system later known as the Spanish Inquisition.

During the Middle Ages, the Catholic Church organized the Inquisition—a tribunal (court) that investigated heresy, or acts by members of the Church that went against accepted Church teachings. But under Isabella and Ferdinand, this court system was much more cruel. They expelled from the country those people who did not want to convert to Catholicism. They killed (often by burning them at the stake) those who converted but still practiced their old religion in secret.

As Isabella and Ferdinand increased their power inside Spain, they sought to increase it outside as well. Portuguese explorers had been trying to develop new trade routes to India and the Far East. So when Christopher Columbus, a Portuguese sailor, asked for their help in his plans to reach the Indies by sailing west across the Atlantic Ocean, they agreed. His famous landing on October 12, 1492, on islands in the Caribbean was not exactly what he had set out to do. But it opened the way for Spanish colonization in the New World.

In Western Europe, Ferdinand increased Spanish power when he obtained the kingdom of Naples in southern Italy in 1504. Isabella and Ferdinand gained still further strength for their kingdom by marrying off their children to members of other royal houses in Europe (a famous daughter, Catherine of Aragon, eventually married English King Henry VIII).

The strains of running the monarchy and of bearing five children took their toll on Isabella's health. She became ill in the summer of 1504 and never recovered, dying on November 26 at the age of 53. Upon her death, the rule of Castile passed to her daughter Joanna, known as "the Mad" because she suffered from a mental illness. Joanna was not capable of ruling, so Ferdinand, after negotiating with the Castilian nobility, took over Castile in 1507.

Acquiring the kingdom of Navarre in 1512 was Ferdinand's last achievement for Spain. He died in 1516 and was buried next to Isabella in Granada. Their Spanish kingdom, on the verge of becoming a world empire, was inherited by their grandson, the future Holy Roman emperor Charles V (see **Charles V**).

# Ivan IV, the Terrible

*First Russian Czar*
*Born August 25, 1530*
*Died March 18, 1584*

*"Thousands were murdered during his rages, and for this, he became known as Ivan 'the Terrible.'"*

When Ivan was crowned ruler of Russia in 1547, he demanded to be called "czar," the Russian form of the old Roman title of "Caesar." At the time, Russia was geographically larger than almost all other European states. Its population, however, was small and it was not as technologically advanced as many of the states to its west. With the title of "czar," Ivan hoped his European neighbors would recognize him as a powerful ruler and would respect the Russian nation.

Ivan was well educated, and he wrote poetry, composed music, and designed churches. He even introduced into Russia the movable printing press—developed in Germany less than 100 years before. He began his reign by establishing reforms in the government and by trying to secure peace throughout Russia. Ivan strengthened the position of czar and the state of the country. But his cruel childhood had left scars on his fragile character. When tragic events began to occur, he believed people were plotting against him. He felt tortured and could not control his fits of anger. Thousands were murdered during his rages, and for this, he became known as Ivan "the Terrible."

Born in 1530, Ivan was the son of Helena Glinskaya and Vasily III, the Grand Prince of Moscow. Vasily died in 1533 and the three-year-old Ivan was declared Grand Prince. His mother died (probably poisoned) when he was eight, and his happy childhood came to an end. The great Russian nobles, *boyars*, then fought among themselves to gain control over Ivan and the government. Andrei Shuiski, a leading *boyar,* seized power and threw his opponents into dungeons, starving them to death.

Ivan's fate was not much better: he was basically a prisoner in the palace, poorly clothed and fed. Under the kind direction of Metropolitan Makari (Bishop of Moscow), Ivan escaped his misery by reading history, literature, and theology. He learned to hate the *boyars,* but from them he learned how to be cruel. When he was thirteen, he had the unguarded Shuiski arrested, strangled, and his body thrown to the dogs. Over the next few years, Ivan continued his studies while watching the *boyars* struggle for power around him.

## Declared Czar of All Russias

Ivan's study of history, especially that of the Roman Empire, convinced him that Moscow could become another Rome ruled by a Caesar. So in January of 1547, at the age of 16, he had himself crowned Grand Prince and Czar of all the Russias. This was an open challenge to all the *boyars* that he would control power throughout the country. A month later he married Anastasia Romanovna, his first of what eventually would be seven wives. Following his Roman dream, Ivan set out to reform and restructure the Russian government. To further oppose the *boyars,* he assembled a national council, the *Zemski Sobor,* that helped him establish a new legal code to solve the country's social problems.

Having begun his reforms, Ivan gathered his army and moved against Kazan, the capital of the Tartar stronghold on the Volga River east of Moscow. Tartars were Turks that helped the Mongols overrun Asia in the thirteenth century (see

**Alexander Nevsky**). In 1552 Ivan and his army captured Kazan. To celebrate his conquest, he ordered the building of St. Basil's Cathedral: nine churches grouped together, their onion-shaped domes swirled with different colors. Four years later he captured the southern Tartar stronghold of Astrakhan. The Volga, an important trade route to the Caspian Sea, was now controlled by the Russians.

Ivan's advisors wanted him to attack the hostile Tartars living in the Crimea, the southern peninsula of present-day Ukraine. In 1558 Ivan chose instead to invade Livonia (present-day Latvia and Estonia), whose German rulers had prevented foreign craftsmen from reaching Russia. It was a costly error. For the first two years the Russians were victorious and Livonia seemed certain to fall. But neighboring European nations did not want Ivan to have control over the important seaports in this area. Denmark, Poland, and Sweden came to the aid of Livonia and divided it among themselves. The war waged on until 1582 when Ivan finally was forced to sign a treaty giving back any territory the Russians had gained. He even lost to Sweden the lands the Russians already owned along the Gulf of Finland.

## Believes Tragedies Caused by Treason

During this long campaign, personal tragedies struck Ivan. In August 1560, his wife Anastasia died. Within three years, his new wife's son, his brother Yuri, and Metropolitan Makari were all dead. In 1564 his most trusted aide, Andrew Kurbsky, defected to Poland. Believing the *boyars* were responsible for these murders, plots, and even defeats in battle, Ivan arrested and killed many of them. In 1565 he set aside the *Oprichnina,* a section of land that became his personal property. To add to the *Oprichnina,* Ivan then created the *Oprichniki,* a guard of men who seized the lands of disloyal *boyars,* often killing them in the process. As the lands of the *Oprichnina* grew, the number of *boyars* fell. Many others fled the country leaving vast areas of Russia empty.

When Maria, his second wife, died in 1569, Ivan suspected whole cities of being part of a plot. Terror ran through the land, and chaos through the government. Sensing this, the Crimean Tartars struck Moscow in August 1571, burning everything in their path. Only the Kremlin (the fortress of government buildings) remained. Ivan crushed the Tartars when they returned the following August, and for a time he was hailed as a savior. He abolished the *Oprichnina* in 1572, but his fears of treason and plots returned with losses on the Livonian battlefields. In 1581, in a moment of rage, he struck and killed his son and heir, Ivan Ivanovich. Of all the losses Ivan the Terrible suffered, this was his most tragic. Never fully recovering, he fell dead less than three years later.

# Joan of Arc

*French saint and national heroine*

*Born c. 1412,*
*Domremy, France*

*Died May 30, 1431,*
*Rouen, France*

*"The English were eager to prove that Joan could have defeated them only by using witchcraft."*

J oan of Arc is the most famous fighting woman in European history. On the battlefield, she motivated her troops to drive the enemies from her homeland. Although she knew nothing about warfare, she claimed to be guided by visions of saints. Few people believed her; many thought she used sorcery. When Joan's enemies captured her, they declared her a witch and burned her at the stake. Yet her inspiration lived on after her death. She had fought for her king and her country as a whole. This was a new idea to the people at that time, and it helped unite them in victory. Afterward, many came to believe that, indeed, she was divinely led.

Joan was born about 1412 in the village of Domremy, in the Champagne district of northeastern France. As the daughter of a farmer, she grew up herding cattle and sheep, and helping in the fields during the harvest. She did not go to school and never learned to read or to write. Like most peasants in her time, Joan was religious and spent much time praying to the statues of saints that stood around the church in her village.

At the time of Joan's birth, France and England were engaged in a long period of conflict known as the Hundred Years' War. Although this conflict was not really a war, it lasted for more than 100 years. From 1337 to 1453, the two sides fought a series of separate battles over the territory of Aquitaine, a rich land in southwestern France. England had gained control of this area in the twelfth century and was determined not to lose it. France was equally determined to drive the English away from it.

In 1420, after England had won some important battles and gained control of territory in northwestern France, the English and French signed the Treaty of Troyes. This treaty allowed King Henry V of England to become king of France when Charles VI, the current French king, died. Two years later, though, both Henry and Charles died. Charles VII, son of the French king, proclaimed himself heir to the throne. But the French people would not recognize him as king until he was crowned in the cathedral in the English-controlled city of Reims (the traditional site where French kings were crowned).

Trying to capture territory that rightfully belonged to Charles, the English soon broke the Treaty of Troyes by invading central France. In 1428 they attacked the city of Orleans, about eighty miles south of Paris. A victory here would have allowed the English a chance to control all of southern France. But they were stopped by the French, who were led by a seventeen-year-old peasant girl—Joan.

## Voices Tell Her to Lead Army

From about age 13, Joan would later claim, she began having visions of St. Michael (captain-general of the armies of Heaven), St. Catherine, and St. Margaret (both early Christian martyrs). Joan believed the saints told her to drive the English away from Orleans and out of the country, and to take Charles VII to Reims to be crowned. In 1429, after repeated visions, Joan went to the commander of the French army at Vancoulers to explain her mission. He was doubtful at first, but finally sent her—dressed in soldier's clothes—to Charles. Joan soon convinced Charles that God had sent her to save France. She reportedly did this by revealing to him secrets that he believed were known only to himself and to God.

Charles gave Joan a suit of white armor. Legend states that her sword came from the church of Saint Catherine of Fierbois. Even though she had never been there, she told her attendants the sword could be found behind the alter, and it was. Joan then led a group of French soldiers against the English at Orleans. She was wounded, but fought on. Her courage inspired her soldiers to drive the English from the city. Because of this victory, Joan became known as the Maid of Orleans. After a few more battles in which her army cleared the English from the surrounding Loire valley, Joan brought Charles to Reims for his coronation on July 17, 1429.

## Captured and Tried as a Witch

Charles later decided that he wanted to negotiate with the English and the Burgundians, people of an independent state within France who were allies of the English. Joan, on the other hand, wanted France for the French, and she fought on. But she soon lost a few battles. In May of 1430, during the battle of Compiègne, Joan was captured by the Burgundians. She was then sold to the English for 10,000 pounds, taken to the city of Rouen, and shackled to a dungeon wall.

The English were eager to prove that Joan could have defeated them only by using witchcraft. They brought her to trial for sorcery and heresy (the act of challenging the authority of the Church). The representatives of the Church who tried her believed that God would speak only to priests. They wanted her to deny that she had heard the voices of the saints and to remove the soldier's, or men's, clothes that she wore, since this was a violation of Church rules. But Joan refused to do what they wanted.

Charles, whom Joan had helped crown, sent no one to rescue her. After months in prison, sick and weak, she finally signed a general statement of faults and put on women's clothes. The authorities had promised Joan that she could attend church and confession after she had signed this statement. But afterward, they would not let her leave the dungeon;

they had lied to her. In response, Joan put on her soldier's clothes once more. For this disobedience, she was quickly sentenced to death, and on May 30, 1431, she was burned at the stake in the marketplace of Rouen.

The shameful story of her death led everyone involved to try *not* to take the blame. Even Charles tried twice to have the verdict against her overturned. In 1456, a mere 25 years later, Pope Calixtus III declared that Joan had been not guilty, and condemned the verdict against her. In 1920, almost 500 years after her death, the Catholic Church canonized Joan, or declared her to be a saint.

# John XXIII

*Pope*

*Born November 21, 1881,*
*Sotto il Monte, Italy*

*Died June 3, 1963,*
*Vatican, Vatican City*

*"John XXIII sought to unify people in the modern world by bringing them back to the Catholic Church."*

Pope John XXIII came to the papal throne at a time when society was undergoing vast changes. By the middle of the twentieth century, scientists had begun to reach out to explore space. Discoveries in medicine and biology gave people the ability to live longer and a greater understanding of how humans developed and evolved. But this technological progress also brought grave dangers. A new type of war, the cold war, had developed between the superpowers—the Soviet Union and the United States. The world was threatened with total nuclear destruction, and people were growing further and further apart. John XXIII sought to unify people in the modern world by bringing them back to the Catholic Church. By reforming the practices of the Church, he hoped to return it to the center of Western society.

Born Angelo Roncalli in 1881, he was the son of poor peasant farmers in northern Italy. Studying for the priesthood was the only avenue then open for intelligent peasant children. And since young Roncalli was gifted, he was sent to seminary schools in the Italian province of Bergamo and in Rome. In 1904 he received his doctorate in theology and was ordained a priest. For the next ten years, he served as secretary to the bishop of Bergamo. He also taught in the seminary there and wrote many works on church history. During World War I, he served in the medical corps and as a chaplain to several medical hospitals.

In 1925 Roncalli was promoted to archbishop and sent to work as the pope's representative first in Bulgaria and then nine years later in Istanbul, Turkey. Both of these were difficult assignments since Christians were in the minority in both places. But Roncalli stressed harmony. He kept on good terms not only with the Catholics under his care but also with the members of other faiths and of all political parties. In these settings Roncalli gradually developed the diplomatic and organizational skills that would later serve him well.

Roncalli's good work brought him to the attention of the new pope, Pius XII. In 1944, near the end of the Second World War, the pope sent Roncalli to Paris, France, as papal nuncio (highest-ranking representative of the pope). Again he had to show diplomatic skill, this time in bringing together those Catholics who had opposed the Nazis during the war with those who had helped them. Again he was successful, and in 1953 the pope made him a cardinal and gave him the title of patriarch of Venice, an important appointment within the Catholic Church. Though Roncalli disagreed with the communist and socialist parties then in power in Italy, he remained friendly with representatives of each.

## Elected Pope

Roncalli's final promotion came on October 25, 1958, when he was named the new pope. Although he was elected because of his great diplomatic skills, he was in his late seventies and people believed he would serve simply and quietly. But this would not be the case. He immediately asserted his independence by choosing the name "John," which had not been used by a pope in over 500 years. He also made the papal office more open, less dependent on formality and ceremony.

He visited schools, hospitals, and prisons in Rome. And he met with many leaders of other religions, including the head of the Greek Orthodox Church and the archbishop of Canterbury. He almost doubled the number of cardinals, including naming the first ones from India and Africa.

Concerned about the rising political problems in the world, John XXIII issued in 1961 a papal letter, *Mater et Magistra (Mother and Teacher)*. He did not favor Western capitalism over communism, but criticized both. He wanted social reforms that expanded human freedoms rather than those that limited them, even if this meant using certain socialist programs. He also appealed to wealthy nations to help those that were underdeveloped. John XXIII's social concerns went even further in another papal letter, *Pacem in terris (Peace on Earth)*, issued in 1963. This letter was directed not just to Catholics but to all good people in the world. In it he urged the powerful nations to make peace and to rid the world of the dangers of nuclear war.

Pope John XXIII's most important achievement, however, was his decision to call together an ecumenical (Greek for "universal") council of church leaders to change Church teachings. This was the twenty-first time in the history of the Catholic Church that such a group had gathered. John XXIII gave this council, called the Second Vatican Council, the task of adapting the Church to the modern world and rebuilding its reputation. The council met on October 11, 1962, and in the autumn of each year until 1965.

## Council Modernizes Church

When the Second Vatican Council had finished, the Church had a new direction. Relations with members of other Christian faiths, such as Protestantism, were opened and strengthened. Members of the clergy, especially bishops, were given less administrative duties and directed to work more with church members. The most important change, however, was the increased involvement of the laity (the common members who belonged to the Church). Catholic services used to be conducted only in Latin. Now they were led in everyday language. Not only could the laity better understand the service, but they actually took part in it (such as helping with communion). They were also allowed to become members of councils that decided on issues important to their particular parish or church.

Although these important reforms brought about Pope John XXIII's desire to have the Church enter the modern world, he did not live long enough to see it happen. He died from gastric cancer on June 3, 1963. He had sat on the papal throne for only four and one-half years, less than any pope before him in the twentieth century. But his fresh approach and his dedication to the welfare of all people made him popular. Throughout the world, his death was mourned by Catholics and non-Catholics alike. In 1965 Pope Paul VI began the process to have John XXIII declared a saint.

# Vladimir Lenin

*Russian revolutionary, founder of the Soviet Union*

*Born April 22, 1870, Simbirsk, Russia*

*Died January 21, 1924, Nizhni Novgorod, U.S.S.R. (present-day Russia)*

*"Lenin firmly believed that what he did was best for his countrymen."*

Vladimir Lenin was one of the greatest revolutionary leaders of all time. He was the founder of the Russian Communist Party and the moving force behind the Russian Revolution of 1917. The government he created formed the Union of Soviet Socialist Republics (U.S.S.R.), better known as the Soviet Union. This federal republic lasted for 69 years and deeply influenced the history of the entire modern world. In the few years he controlled the government, he ruled like a dictator, and those who opposed him suffered. But Lenin did not change the course of Russian history because he sought power and glory—he firmly believed that what he did was best for his countrymen.

He was born Vladimir Ilyich Ulyanov in 1870 in Simbursk, a city on the Volga River (he adopted the revolutionary name "Lenin" when he was an adult). He was the son of Ilya Ulyanov, a school administrator, and Maria Alexandrovna Blank. Although his childhood was happy and uneventful, he suffered two tragedies when he was a teenager. In 1886 his father died from a cerebral hemorrhage. The following year his brother Alexander, a university student, was arrested and hanged for plotting to murder Czar Alexander III.

The Russian people suffered under the czar. Although he had abolished serfdom, or the practice of using peasant farmers as slaves, he still ruled the country with unlimited power. Even worse, he persecuted anyone who disagreed with his policies. Influenced by the spread of Marxism, a theory and practice where workers control business and government (see **Karl Marx**), people in Russia wanted a greater voice in government and began rebelling. Lenin became a part of this rebellion while he was a law student at the University of Kazan. Although he was expelled because of his politics, he continued to study on his own and passed the exams to become a lawyer in 1891.

## Lenin Exiled to Siberia

Two years later Lenin moved to St. Petersburg, then the capital of Russia. He joined a Marxist movement and met Nadezhda Krupskaya. His seriousness about being a revolutionary caused the other members in the movement to call him Starik, "the old one." In 1895 Lenin was arrested along with dozens of his companions (including Krupskaya), sent to prison for fourteen months, and then banished to Siberia (northern region of Russia) for three years. While in Siberia, he married Krupskaya. The couple settled in Switzerland after their exile in Siberia ended in 1900.

Lenin continued his revolutionary activities. In 1902 he wrote a pamphlet, *What Is to Be Done?*, stating that only professional revolutionaries could bring about socialism (a political system where workers controlled businesses and the government). The following year Russian Marxists met in London to set up a unified political party. But they soon broke into two groups: those that agreed with Lenin's views were called Bolsheviks ("those of the majority"), while those who disagreed were called Mensheviks ("those of the minority").

Revolution broke out in Russia in 1905. A crowd of workers, seeking changes in labor laws, marched on the czar's palace and were fired on by troops. Hundreds of people were killed. Riots, strikes, and other outbreaks followed over the next few months before order was restored. Although Lenin went to Russia, he was too late to take part in the uprising. He returned to Switzerland, determined to continue the fight for socialism. In 1912, at another meeting of Russian Marxists, he broke with his opponents and officially formed the independent Bolshevik Party.

Lenin's stand on World War I further separated him from other Marxists. Begun in 1914, the war pitted Russia, France, and England against Germany and Austria-Hungary. Many Russians supported the war, but Lenin did not. He believed a defeat for Russia would help bring about the revolution he wanted. In the beginning Lenin found little support for his views. But the war soon changed the Russian people's minds. By 1917 they were tired of fighting and had very little to eat. In March, in the city of Petrograd (formerly St. Petersburg), workers went on strike and began rioting for more food. The military, also hungry, refused to shoot the workers and joined the revolution. After a few weeks, the palace was captured and Czar Nicholas II was forced to give up the throne.

## Bolsheviks Seize the Government

A provisional, or temporary, government was set up under the leadership of Alexander Kerensky. Although he kept Russia in the war, Kerensky failed to solve the country's urgent economic problems. Lenin, therefore, wanted the provisional government removed and power given to political organizations of workers, peasants, and soldiers called soviets (Russian word for council). An uprising against the government in July was quickly put down, and Lenin was forced to flee to Finland. He soon returned, however, and formed the Red Guard, a militia of factory workers. With the help of this Guard, Lenin and the Bolsheviks overthrew the government in November.

The Bolsheviks (who changed their name to the Communist party) were now in control. Lenin immediately sought to end the war with Germany, and in March 1918 Russia signed the Treaty of Brest-Litovsk. Although this unfair treaty gave huge sections of Russia to Germany, Lenin convinced his people it was necessary to end the war. Following this, Lenin's government seized privately owned lands and gave them to the peasants. It also gave workers control over factories. And to silence any opposition, the government formed a secret police force, the *Cheka*.

This wasn't enough to stop a civil war. Beginning in 1918 anti-communists (called "Whites") formed armies to fight the communists (called "Reds"). Few lives had been lost in the November revolution, but thousands died in the civil war. Atrocities (acts of brutality) were committed by both sides, and the Russian land was devastated. But the Red Army, led by Leon Trotsky, proved too much for the Whites, and by 1921 the civil war was over.

Trying to help Russia recover from years of revolution and civil war, Lenin began the New Economic Policy (NEP) in 1921. During the civil war, the government took control of almost everything. But the NEP allowed private owners to run small businesses and peasants to sell their farm products to other Russians. While this improved economic conditions in Russia, the political situation remained harsh. Lenin put leaders of all rival groups on trial; no one could question the policies of the Communist government.

On December 30, 1922, the Communist party established the Union of Soviet Socialist Republics. It became the first state formed on Marx's principles of socialism, something for which Lenin had fought many years. But he did not live very long to enjoy it. He suffered the first of a series of strokes beginning in May of 1922. Less than two years later, he was dead. To honor Lenin, the Soviet government put his body on permanent display in a red marble-and-granite mausoleum on Red Square in Moscow.

# Louis XIV

*French king*

*Born September 5, 1638,*
*St. Germain-en-Laye, France*

*Died September 1, 1715,*
*Versailles, France*

*"With his magnificent, showy manner, surrounded by art and artists, Louis ... became known as the 'Sun King.'"*

Under the reign of Louis XIV, France reached the height of power in Europe, although everything Louis did for the country he did for himself. As a child, he had been told he was chosen by God to be the king of France. As he grew older, he came to believe firmly that the French state could not exist without him. His famous statement, "L'É-tat, c'est moi" ("I am the state") best represented his belief. He sought to glorify France, then, by glorifying himself. The palace he had built was fit for a god, and its theme was Apollo, the Greek god of the sun. With his magnificent, showy manner, surrounded by art and artists, Louis became known as the "Sun King."

Louis was the son of King Louis XIII of France and Anne of Austria. When his father died in 1643, he became Louis XIV, king of France. Since he was only four years old, his mother and her chief advisor, Jules Mazarin, ran the government. Until he was seven years old, Louis practiced being king, playing with drums and toy soldiers in the courtyard.

Then his formal education began under the direction of Mazarin. By the time Louis was 12, he could write elegant French and speak Italian, Latin, and Spanish. In addition, he learned horsemanship, fencing, dancing, and other skills fitting a future king. He even was allowed to sit in on official meetings to see how the government worked.

Louis's childhood was not perfect. He contracted smallpox at the age of nine. Because medical treatments were primitive then, he nearly died. Less than a year later, Louis was exposed to the horrors of civil war. Between 1648 and 1653, France was threatened by a series of popular revolts known as the *Fronde*. The Parliament of Paris (the high court) and jealous nobles rose up, trying to gain more power in the kingdom. Louis and his mother were in such danger that one night they had to be secretly taken out of Paris and hidden in a nearby town. That night, the young king slept on a bed of straw, an experience he never forgot. Afterward, he vowed to strengthen the kingship and rule forcefully over all the French people.

After his crowning in 1654 Louis became more interested in women than in the government. When he almost died from typhoid fever in 1658, he realized he had to marry and produce an heir to carry on the French crown. The prime candidate was Princess Marie Thérèse of Spain. Since France and Spain had poor relations, this marriage would help secure peace between them. Although he loved another woman, Louis married Marie Thérèse in 1660 for the betterment of his kingdom.

## Builds Palace at Versailles

Louis's dedication to France was now clear. When Mazarin died in 1661, Louis decided not to have an advisor. He also replaced most of the nobles in government offices with learned and trustworthy people. This ensured not only that the government would be more efficient but that everyone answered to Louis. To provide a symbol of his might and authority, Louis had a glorious palace built at Versailles, outside of Paris. Designed mainly by the architects Charles le Brun and Jean Hardouin-Mansart, the palace was surrounded by elaborate gardens and 1,400 fountains and housed up to 10,000 people. The king himself became a majestic presence at Versailles. Handing Louis his nightshirt or holding his candle at bedtime were considered great honors. These elaborate rituals, combined with the magnificent works of art and architectural details in the palace, made for a brilliant court life at Versailles.

The Catholic Louis saw himself as a reformer. To unify the country under one religion, he attacked the Huguenots, or French Protestants. The Edict of Nantes (edict means order) in 1598 had given the Huguenots the right to practice their religion without fear of abuse. But Louis canceled this edict in 1685 and began forcing the Huguenots to convert to Catholicism. Many fled the country, robbing France of important businessmen and skilled craftsman. Other reforms, however, strengthened France. Louis regulated the laws and expanded industry and commerce. He also encouraged the arts, making France the cultural center of the Western world. Many writers, such as Jean Baptiste Molière and Jean Racine, prospered under Louis's support.

## Establishes Power in Europe

Although France claimed a large part of North America (from Québec to Louisiana) at this time, Louis wanted glory in Europe. So he reorganized his military, making it more disciplined, bigger, and better supplied. Seeking to widen France's territory, Louis began a series of battles with the Netherlands beginning in 1667. Although he did not completely defeat the Dutch, by 1678 he had gained the county of Burgundy between France and Switzerland and some smaller regions near present-day Belgium. This, however, did not satisfy him and he sought more territory around France. Unfortunately for Louis, a group of European countries—including Spain, Sweden, the Netherlands, and England—formed an alliance known as the League of Augsburg to stop him. The resulting war lasted from 1688 to 1697. Neither side gained much, but Louis had established himself as a dominant power by standing up to almost everyone in Europe.

Louis's personal life was equally eventful. Although married to Marie Thérèse, Louis had many mistresses and fathered many children. When his wife died in 1683, Louis secretly married Françoise Maintenon, who had been the governess of his illegitimate children. After this marriage, however, his life changed. Maintenon's moral attitude had a great calming effect on Louis and his court. And life at Versailles became more dignified.

Louis's desire to expand French power hurt his kingdom in the end. When the Spanish king Charles II died in 1700, Louis, as Charles's brother-in-law, hoped his children would inherit the powerful Spanish empire. But some League of Augsburg nations—now known as the Grand Alliance—refused to have the French and Spanish crowns joined, and war broke out. The War of Spanish Succession weakened France's military and economy, and in 1713 Louis was forced to sign the Treaty of Utrecht. This treaty gave the Spanish throne to Louis's grandson Philip V, but destroyed Louis's idea of a combined French and Spanish crown. France kept its conquered territories in Europe and remained a great power in the eighteenth century. Louis died two years later, leaving the throne to his five-year-old great-grandson, Louis XV.

# Martin Luther

*German leader of Protestant Reformation*

*Born November 10, 1483,*
*Eisleben, Saxony, present-day Germany*

*Died February 18, 1546,*
*Eisleben, Saxony*

*"Luther had defended his beliefs by stating that people should live their lives by following the Bible, not the pope."*

The world into which Martin Luther was born on November 10, 1483, was in the midst of great change. In Western European history, the Middle Ages (roughly from 400 to 1400) had been an age of walls and of faith. Around each little town men had built massive stone walls against the evils outside. Inside these walls, medieval people knew their place. They were craftsmen, noblemen, churchmen, farmers, and knights. They did not question their duties because they were safe and had faith in the way things were run.

In the fifteenth and sixteenth centuries, however, men and women began to peer beyond these walls. Geographical revelations, like Christopher Columbus's discovery of the New World in 1492, opened people's view of the world. And scientific revelations, like Polish astronomer Nicholas Copernicus's theory that the earth revolved around the sun, opened people's view of the heavens. People began using their own reasoning to find truths. It was an age of exploration and of reformation, or change. Before, people came to know God only through the Church. Now they, including Luther, sought a better way to understand God by themselves.

Young Luther was raised in a household that was very strict and very religious. His parents, Hans and Margaret Luther, were peasants and uneducated. But they recognized their son's gifted ability as a student and encouraged him to study hard. In 1501 Luther enrolled at the University of Erfurt, one of the oldest and most respected universities in Germany. In just four years, he earned both his B.A. and M.A. degrees. He then began studying law.

## Thunderstorm Changes Life

On a hot and muggy July day in 1505, Luther's life took a different path. While walking down a country road, he was caught in a sudden thunderstorm. When lightening stuck nearby, he became frightened and cried out to his patron saint: "Save me, Saint Anne, and I will become a monk." Luther lived through the storm and, two weeks later, entered an Augustinian monastery. Here life was strict. In addition to studying the Bible intensely, Luther had to perform hard tasks, such as scrubbing floors and barns. Finally, in 1507 he was ordained a priest. The following year he went to the University of Wittenberg to further his religious studies and to lecture on the teachings of the ancient Greek philosopher Aristotle.

Luther was a deeply troubled man. The medieval Church taught that people could only overcome their sinfulness by constantly doing good deeds and by taking part in rituals of the Church, such as baptism and communion. Only then would people receive God's grace. This disturbed Luther, for no matter how hard he worked at earning his salvation, he could not find any peace. God, it seemed to Luther, was vengeful and demanded too much. Then one day, while studying the Bible, Luther read "The just shall live by faith." He interpretted this statement to mean that God only required people to have faith. Nothing else mattered. Luther concluded that people did not need the ceremonies of the Church.

What made Luther openly challenge the Church, though, was its practice of selling indulgences, or pardons for sins. It was believed that Jesus Christ, the Virgin Mary, and the many Christian saints filled a vast treasury in heaven with infinite merits they had earned through their goodness and suffering. The pope was able to "borrow" quantities of this goodness and give them to people who were repentant, or sorry for their mistakes. Repentant sinners were given indulgences whenever they viewed saintly relics. But the pope also allowed priests to sell indulgences in order to make money for the Church. People could buy them for sins they had already committed or for sins they might yet commit.

## Nails Statements to Church Door

This angered Luther. He thought that indulgences allowed people to keep committing sins. And he believed only God could forgive sins, not the pope. So on October 31, 1517, Luther nailed to the church door in Wittenberg a list of 95 theses, or statements, attacking indulgences. He then invited anyone to debate these statements. It was one and one-half years before Johann Eck, another scholarly monk, accepted Luther's challenge. The debate, in the city of Leipzig, raged on for 18 days before it was called off. Luther had defended his beliefs by stating that people should live their lives by following the Bible, not the pope. He said people could find their own salvation through faith—they did not need the Church.

Luther began writing his views in pamphlets, and his words soon spread throughout Germany. Many people backed him. In June 1520, Pope Leo X issued a document criticizing Luther and excluding him from membership in the Church. When Luther received this document, he publicly burned it. The following April, in the town of Worms, an assembly of German princes (called the Diet) summoned Luther. The Diet wanted Luther to withdraw his views. He refused. So they declared him an outlaw and sentenced him to death. But Frederick the Wise, the prince who ruled Wittenberg and was Luther's friend, kidnapped Luther and hid him in Wartburg Castle. There, over the next eleven months, Luther spent his time translating the New Testament from Latin into German.

Returning to Wittenberg in March 1522, Luther tried to unify his followers. By then, almost half the people of Germany had adopted his views. Many called themselves "Lutherans." Luther introduced many reforms in the form of worship. He placed an emphasis on preaching and teaching from the Bible, and he reintroduced music and congregational singing. A fine musician, Luther wrote many hymns, including "A Mighty Fortress Is Our God" and "Away in a Manger."

In 1525 Luther married Katherine von Bora, a former nun. They had six children and adopted eleven more. Throughout the remaining years of his life, Luther continued writing, preaching, and teaching. He died on February 18, 1546, four days after he had preached in Eisleben, his hometown. He was buried in Wittenberg, in the church on whose door he had posted his "95 Theses."

# Marcus Aurelius

*Roman emperor and philosopher*

*Born April 26, 121,*
*Rome, present-day Italy*

*Died March 17, 180,*
*Vienna, present-day Austria*

*"It was during these years of hardship, among the misty swamps by the Danube, that Marcus wrote the Meditations."*

Before Marcus Aurelius became emperor, the Roman Empire had enjoyed long years of peace. It controlled a vast area of land, from Europe and north Africa in the west to Turkey and Syria in the east. But for 16 of the 19 years of his rule, Marcus had to battle various tribes living in this great area who rose up against the authority of the Empire. Although he won most of the battles he fought and held together the Empire, he was not a soldier. He valued life too much to enjoy taking it. In the gloomy hours after battles, Marcus wrote in his journal his thoughts about life and death. He tried to live his own life by the noble and humble thoughts he wrote down. This journal, now known as the *Meditations*, has inspired generations and has become one of the world's most famous books.

Marcus was born on April 26, 121, during the rule of the emperor Hadrian. Both of his parents died when he was young, and he was adopted by his grandfather, Annius Verus. His childhood was happy; he enjoyed riding, hunting, wrestling, and outdoor games. But Marcus was also very studious. At the age of seven, he began his formal schooling with tutors. He studied Greek and Latin, literature, and public speaking. As he grew older, his studies included Roman law, mathematics, music, painting, and philosophy. Marcus became so attracted to the study of philosophy, in fact, that he eagerly tried to follow the strict lifestyle of philosophers: often he would wear a rough tunic and sleep on the ground. It was during these later studies that Marcus learned about Stoic philosophy. He would try to live by its principles throughout his life.

When Marcus was seventeen, Hadrian became very ill. But his successor, Commodus, died before him. So Hadrian chose Antoninus Pius to become the next emperor. Antoninus's wife, Faustina, was Marcus's aunt. Since Antoninus did not have a son, he adopted both Marcus and Lucius Verus, Commodus's son. Antoninus changed Marcus's name to Marcus Aurelius Antoninus and made him his successor. He then gave his daughter, also named Faustina, to Marcus to marry. During their marriage, Faustina would bear five children, but only one would live to adulthood. That son, Commodus, would eventually succeed Marcus as emperor.

## Stoicism

This school of philosophy was founded around 300 B.C. by Zeno of Citium (a city in Cyprus). Stoicism got its name from Zeno's habit of lecturing his followers in Athens, Greece, at the painted "stoa," a covered porch lined with columns . The Stoics believed there existed in the universe a guiding force (God, Nature, Fate) that was not separate, but lived in all things. This force was alive and intelligent, and it directed the growth of things toward their proper end. The chief end of man—his highest good—was happiness. And happiness could be achieved by "living according to Nature," or this universal force. The Stoics thought this universal force existed in man through his reason (intellect), his highest principle. Thus, they felt that man must be ethical and live according to his reason, not his passions. Only then would he find happiness.

At the mere age of eighteen, Marcus became consul (an official who managed the city and commanded the army), the highest elected officer in Rome. Over the next 22 years, Marcus prepared himself to take over the Empire by learning the rules and the workings of the government. He also began a deeper study of Stoic philosophy. Its teachings that men must calmly accept and respond to whatever destiny might bring would serve Marcus well during his future role as emperor.

## Shares Throne with Adopted Brother

Marcus was proclaimed emperor on March 7, 161, after the death of Antoninus. He immediately made Lucius Verus his partner on the throne. It was the first time the Roman Empire was ruled by two emperors at the same time. Marcus and Lucius were enormously popular with Roman citizens from the beginning and remained so throughout their lives. They began a government institution that cared for poor children. They appointed only worthy judges and magistrates. They even had the roads repaired.

But crises soon struck their reign. That autumn the Tiber River, which runs through Rome, flooded. The harvest failed and famine spread. Then Parthia, an ancient kingdom in what is now Iran, invaded territory controlled by the Romans. Marcus sent his armies to reclaim this land. They defeated the Parthians, but when the troops returned in 166 they brought back a plague, a highly contagious disease. It quickly spread throughout the Roman world, killing many people.

That same year German tribes crossed over the Danube, a river that begins in the Black Forest mountains of Germany and empties into the Black Sea, and attacked the Empire in northern Italy. Since the plague had reduced the size of the Roman army, Marcus could not fight with full strength. In addition, the plague had damaged the economy of Rome. But Marcus refused to raise taxes. Instead, he sold the Empire's jewelry and other property in order to feed the army. Marcus had to fight these tribes on and off for the next 14 years. In 169, Lucius died, and Marcus was left to lead his troops alone.

It was during these years of hardship that Marcus wrote the *Meditations*. He remained true to his Stoic ideals: he accepted his difficulties with patience. Since he believed all men were connected by the universal force, he was merciful even to his enemies. When members of his own army rebelled against him, he did not kill them. He gave them only a light punishment. Still trying to maintain the Empire, Marcus died on March 17, 180, after a disease had swept through his camp.

# Margaret I

*Queen of Denmark, Norway, and Sweden*

*Born 1353*

*Died 1412*

From the ninth through the eleventh centuries, groups of Vikings terrorized areas of Western Europe seeking power and land. They often intermarried with the natives in the areas they conquered, producing new ethnic groups such as the Normans in France. At first, the Vikings who remained in their Scandinavian homelands were isolated bands without a national identity. By the eleventh century rulers had formed three separate kingdoms: Denmark, Norway, and Sweden. Denmark and Norway briefly came together in the eleventh century under the reign of King Canute (see **Canute I, the Great**). But these three Scandinavian kingdoms basically remained separate until the end of the fourteenth century when they were united by Margaret Valdemarsdottir.

Margaret, the daughter of Helvig and King Waldemar IV of Denmark, was born in 1353. Little is known of her childhood. Typically, the role of noble girls of her time was simply to take part in political marriages. Hers was no different. When she was 10 years old, her father arranged for her to

*"The strong, unified Scandinavia that Margaret created was one of the largest empires in Europe."*

marry 23-year-old King Haakon VI of Norway. Through this marriage, Waldemar secured a treaty with Haakon's father, Magnus VII, who had taken over the kingships of both Norway and Sweden earlier in the century.

Soon after the marriage, Waldemar's son Christopher died. Margaret, queen of Norway and heir to her father-in-law's kingdom in Sweden, now also became heir to her father's kingdom in Denmark. The possibility of one person governing all three kingdoms alarmed the Hanseatic League, a powerful business alliance of German cities that controlled trade throughout Scandinavia. In 1370 the League forced Waldemar to sign an agreement that gave the German merchant cities the power to decide who would be his successor. Poor relations between the League and Scandinavian kings would continue far beyond Margaret's reign.

## Wins Kingship for Son

By the time Margaret was 18, she had borne her only child, Olaf. Five years later, in 1375, Waldemar died, and Margaret tried to have Olaf elected king of Denmark. But her nephew, Albert, took the title of king, claiming Waldemar had promised the throne to him. Albert had not been elected by the Danish nobility, however, and Margaret convinced the Hanseatic League to give its consent to the crowning of her son. Only 23 years old, she showed great political insight in having her son elected King Olaf V of Denmark.

When Haakon died in 1380, Margaret immediately went to Norway to make sure Olaf gained his father's kingdom. Thus began a union between Denmark and Norway that was to last for over four centuries until 1814. Since Olaf was still young, Margaret became his regent (person who governs in the place of a ruler). With the Hanseatic League controlling important areas in Denmark, Margaret had to focus her attention there while at the same time watching over Norway. She forcefully managed both countries.

After Magnus VII died in 1374, the crown of Sweden had been taken over by his nephew Albert of Mecklenburg. Haakon had died believing the Swedish throne rightfully belonged to him. So when Olaf came of age in 1385 and began to rule Denmark and Norway alone, Margaret convinced him that he was the proper successor to the kingship in Sweden. But before he could act in Sweden, Olaf died suddenly in 1387.

## Rules All of Scandinavia

Margaret was now alone. But she was determined not to give up her roles in the governments of Denmark and Norway, and both countries soon declared her to be Olaf's rightful heir. Thus, she became the first medieval queen to rule in Europe. Her position now strengthened, she sought the crown of Sweden. The Swedish nobility, angered by Albert's dealings with the Germans, appealed to her for help. In 1389, Margaret fought and captured Albert near Falkoping, Sweden. She was now ruler over three kingdoms.

Margaret wanted a unified Scandinavian kingdom. To make sure that it would continue, she needed an heir. She chose her great-nephew Erik of Pomerania as her successor. The Norwegians recognized eight-year-old Erik as king in 1389. Seven years later Denmark and Sweden recognized him as well. In 1397 Margaret gathered nobles from all three countries together at a meeting in Kalmar, Sweden. Here Erik was officially crowned. A pact, the Kalmar Union, was drawn up to thoroughly unify the three countries under one king. Margaret hoped to establish a dynasty, where her descendants would automatically inherit the crown. But the nobles wanted to keep the right to elect each king, so the pact was never officially accepted by all three countries.

Even though Erik became old enough to rule in 1400, Margaret remained in control of the combined kingdoms until her death in 1412. Within that time she changed the way the governments in the countries were run. Before, each country was controlled by a king inside that country. But Margaret governed Norway and Sweden from Denmark. She filled many government offices in those two countries with Danish nobles, angering Norwegians and Swedes. Regardless, she maintained control. The strong, unified Scandinavia that Margaret created was one of the largest empires in Europe. But it was not long lasting. Because of disagreements among the three countries, the union was dissolved just over 100 years later.

# Karl Marx

*Prussian social philosopher and writer*

*Born May 5, 1818,*
*Trier, Prussia*

*Died March 14, 1883,*
*London, England*

*"Marx is known as the father of modern communism."*

Karl Marx spent most of his life calling for a social system where everyone would be equal and no one would be poor. Because of his views he was banned from many countries. When he died, he wasn't considered a citizen of any country. Known as Marxism, his ideas inspired the famous Russian Revolution in 1917 (see **Vladimir Lenin**), and they form the basis of many socialist and communist governments in the world today. To many people he is considered a great economic historian. To many others he is known as the father of modern communism.

Marx was born in 1811 in Prussia to Jewish parents. His father, Heinrich Marx, was a lawyer and a Prussian official. In 1815 the Prussian government banned Jews from public office, so Heinrich Marx had his entire family baptized as Protestants. Growing up, the young Marx excelled in the study of languages, especially Latin and French (in his later years he could also read Spanish, Italian, Dutch, Russian, and English). In 1835 his father sent him to the University of Bonn hoping he would become a lawyer. Marx, however, wanted to become a poet and a dramatist, so he studied philosophy and literature. Although he studied very hard, Marx preferred to drink and to fight duels with his fellow students. He also secretly became engaged to Jenny von Westphalen, the daughter of a high government official.

Disgusted with his son's study habits, Heinrich Marx transferred him to the University of Berlin in 1836. This school had higher academic standards and Marx finally took his education seriously. He initially studied law, philosophy, and history, but soon became interested mainly in philosophy. He was influenced by the ideas of the German philosopher Georg Wilhelm Friedrich Hegel.

Hegel believed that reality existed only in the mind, not in the outside world. Ideas were therefore more important than physical things. He thought progress throughout history occurred when two opposing ideas clashed and gave rise to a new, better idea. Marx accepted Hegel's method of thinking, but not his belief in ideas. Marx thought that reality existed in the physical world, and that the struggle between social classes, not ideas, is what has brought about progress.

After completing his studies at Berlin, Marx received his doctorate in 1841 from the University of Jena. He tried to become a teacher, but his political views were extremely non-traditional and no university would hire him. Marx then turned to journalism, and began writing articles for a politically rebellious newspaper, *Rheinische Zeitung,* in the Prussian city of Cologne. Within a year, he became editor. But Prussian officials soon shut down the paper, believing its radical views threatened the government.

## Industrial Revolution Changes Society

Spreading through Europe during this time was the Industrial Revolution, and it changed the way people lived and worked. Before, societies were agrarian—most people lived on farms and worked by hand. The land was owned usually by a noble or a king who granted it to people in exchange for loyalty. This form of society was known as feudalism. But with the increasing use of machines, people began living in cities and working in factories or mills. These factories and large businesses were not run by the government, but were owned and operated by private citizens. Instead of working for nobles or kings, people now worked for the owners of businesses, and the owners made profits from their work. This economic system is called capitalism.

Marx felt there was a great fault in capitalism. He believed most societies were becoming dark and cruel, and that people were unhappy and separated from one another. As industries and businesses grew, the owners became rich. Since they paid very low wages, their workers became poorer and poorer. When Marx spoke out against this inequality in Prussia, he was forced to leave the country in 1843. Before he left, he had married Jenny von Westphalen, and together they settled in Paris.

While in Paris Marx studied philosophy and history, strengthening his ideas against a capitalist-based society. He also met the German philosopher Friedrich Engels, whose father owned successful mills in Prussia and England. Because of the poor conditions he had witnessed in the mills, Engels shared many of Marx's beliefs and became his closest friend. When the French government forced Marx to leave in 1845, Engels followed his friend to Brussels, the capital of Belgium. Here the two men began to publish many of their beliefs.

Marx and Engels developed a theory called historical materialism. They both agreed that history had been shaped by struggles between social classes. Out of these struggles had come new economic systems. The most recent system, capitalism, pitted the wealthy middle class (called the bourgeoisie) against the working class (called the proletariat after the lowest class of citizens in ancient Rome). Marx and Engels predicted that the struggle between the bourgeoisie and the proletariat would result in a system known as socialism, where the means of production and distribution (farms, factories, ships, railroads, stores) would be collectively owned by all the workers. In a sense, people would be working for themselves and for each other, and all people would become workers. There would be no private property and no classes in society because everyone would be equal.

## Writes *Communist Manifesto*

These ideas caught the attention of the Communist League, a political organization of German workers based in London. The League asked Marx and Engels to write its platform, or a statement of what the League stood for. In 1848 this statement was published as the *Communist Manifesto.* In it, Marx and Engels applied their theory of historical materialism in calling for the proletariat to unite in rebellion against the bourgeoisie. After its publication, Marx returned to Cologne to edit another politically radical newspaper, the *Neue rheinische Zeitung.* Again, the government forced him to leave because of his threatening views, such as urging people to resist paying taxes.

This time Marx took his family to London, settling there in 1849. He was unable to find a job, and had to live off the support of Engels. In 1852 he finally found a job as a correspondent for the *New York Daily Tribune.* In addition to his journalism, Marx continued to write on history, economics, and society. He began a huge writing project fully describing not only his beliefs but the history of capitalism and the processes by which it would, he argued, lead to its own decline. Called *Das Kapital,* only one volume of this work was published during his lifetime. Many critics praised the work, and Marx became famous. He was never free from poverty, though, and his family suffered. Four of his seven children died young; two others committed suicide when they were adults. Marx never lived to see the revolution in Russia that his ideas brought about. He died in 1883, two years after his wife.

# Mary, Queen of Scots

*Scottish queen*

*Born December 7 (or 8), 1542, Linlithgow, Scotland*

*Died February 8, 1587, Fotheringhay, England*

Mary, Scotland's most famous queen, has become a romantic and thrilling figure in history. She was born in Scotland but raised in France, where her education made her a true Renaissance princess. Although she returned to rule her Protestant homeland, she remained true to the Catholic ideals of her adopted country. For her courage, charm, and reported beauty, she was admired by many, but she spent the remainder of her life seeking what she and others believed was rightfully hers—the crown of England. This part of her story is filled with bold action, secret plots, and murder.

She was born Mary Stewart on December 7 or 8, 1542, to James V, king of Scotland, and Mary of Guise. A week later, the king was dead, and the baby Mary became queen. Five and one-half years later her mother, related to a powerful French family, arranged for Mary to marry Francis, the young son of the French king, Henry II. Mary went to France and, for the next 10 years, was raised in the Catholic French court. Here she received a wide and refined education: she mastered six languages, including Greek. She studied the histories of great empires and French and Italian poetry. And she learned to dance, sing, and play the lute.

On April 24, 1558, Mary and Francis were married. Over the next two years, events changed her life dramatically. In November of that year, the queen of England, Mary I, died. Her Protestant half-sister Elizabeth I (see **Elizabeth I**) became queen. But many Catholics in Europe did not recognize Elizabeth as the rightful heir to the throne. They thought the marriage of her parents (King Henry VIII and Anne Boleyn) was not legal. They believed the Scottish Mary, as the grandniece of Henry VIII, carried the royal bloodline and should sit on the throne.

In July 1559, Mary's life was further complicated when Henry II died from wounds suffered during a jousting tournament. Francis and Mary were declared king and queen of France. A year later, though, Mary's happiness ended when she learned of her mother's death. Then just six months later, Francis died. Mary was devastated; her health declined. She finally accepted an invitation to return to Scotland to become its ruler. What she truly desired, though, was the crown of England.

## Assumes Rule in Scotland

Mary returned to a far different country from the one she had left 13 years before. Previously tied to the French, Scotland now associated itself with Protestant England. Most of the Scottish people turned against Catholics. The Scottish Parliament had even forbid the celebration of the Catholic Mass. When Mary began her rule she insisted upon having Mass said in her own chapel. But she accepted Protestantism in her country and even approved certain laws against Catholics. The Scottish people looked up to her. She had shown great courage by defending her own beliefs. But she had also shown good will and common sense by accepting policies the majority of people wanted.

In the meantime, Mary tried to secure her right to the English throne by marrying her first cousin Henry Stewart, Lord Darnley, on July 29, 1565. Many Catholics thought

Darnley, as grandnephew of Henry VIII, was next in line to the throne after Mary. But Mary soon tired of Darnley, whom she thought was stupid and arrogant. She refused to give him the crown matrimonial, or a lawful promise that he would have power during her reign.

Darnley, irritated by his wife's neglect, plotted to kill David Rizzio, an Italian musician who had become Mary's most trusted friend (some said lover). On March 9, 1566, a band of nobles dragged the screaming Rizzio from the queen's chamber and stabbed him 56 times. But Mary, who was six months pregnant at the time, regained Darnley's affection. On June 19, 1566, she gave birth to a son, the future King James I of England.

After the birth of their son, Mary's distaste for Darnley only deepened. On February 10, 1567, the house where Darnley had been staying was blown up. His body was found strangled in the garden. Many people believed the murderer was James Hepburn, earl of Bothwell, who was rumored to be Mary's new lover. He was put on trial for the murder, but found not guilty. Then, granted a quick divorce from his wife, he married Mary on May 15, 1567. This last act turned many of Mary's loyal followers against her. A month later, her government was overthrown. On July 24, she was forced to give up the throne in favor of her son.

## Investigated for Murder

In May 1568, Mary escaped to England to seek help from her cousin Elizabeth I. Elizabeth did not trust Mary , however, and had the English government investigate Mary's part in Darnley's murder. At the trial, a collection of letters written by Mary to Bothwell (the "Casket Letters") were presented that supposedly proved her guilt. Although, the court did not find her guilty in the murder plot, she was not allowed to return to Scotland. Instead, she was forced to spend the rest of her life in England.

For the next eighteen years, held captive in cold and drafty castles, Mary planned her escape. Many Catholics, both in Scotland and in England, plotted to put Mary on the English throne. In 1586, a spy for Elizabeth intercepted a letter from Mary to an English Catholic named Anthony Babington. The letter allegedly showed Mary's approval of a plan to assassinate Elizabeth. Mary was then put on trial again. This time she was found guilty of treason and sentenced to die. The grace and courage that had so marked her life also marked her death. On February 8, 1587, Mary's executioner knelt to ask for her forgiveness. She gave it to him before kneeling down to be beheaded.

# Napoleon I Bonaparte

*French emperor*

*Born August 15, 1769,*
*Ajaccio, Corsica*

*Died May 5, 1821,*
*Saint Helena*

*"At the crowning ceremony, Napoleon took the crown from the hands of the pope and placed it on his own head."*

Born on a small island in the Mediterranean Sea, Napoleon Bonaparte rose from a lieutenant in the army to become emperor of the French. Many of the reforms and institutions he set up still exist in the French government and in French society. The empire he created through war and diplomacy was the largest since Roman times. Additionally, he was able to bring to an end the Holy Roman Empire, which had lasted in Europe for almost 850 years. The ideals he fought for in his youth—liberty and equality—passed on to the people in the countries he controlled. This gave rise to nationalism, the idea of a people being united in one nation with one culture, free from the rule of others. It ultimately destroyed his empire, and the man whose reign marked an era in European history died alone, banished to a small island in the Atlantic Ocean.

Born on Corsica in 1769, Napoleon was the son of Letizia Ramolino and Charles Bonaparte, a lawyer. He had four brothers and three sisters, and his close family would remain important to him throughout his life. Most people living on Corsica were of Italian heritage, but the island came under French rule a year before Napoleon's birth. That made him a French citizen. So he entered a military school in Brienne in northeast France when he was ten. He was teased by his classmates because he was small and because he spoke French with an Italian accent. But he was an excellent student, studying history, French literature, and the writings of the Greek philosophers Plato and Aristotle. Because of his mathematical ability, he earned a spot at the famed military academy in Paris in 1784. He graduated a year later, receiving the rank of lieutenant in the French army. When on leave from the army, Napoleon helped his fellow Corsicans work toward independence from France.

The French Revolution broke out in 1789. Because of wars and King Louis XVI's excessive style of living, France was in debt. To find ways to raise money, the king called together the Estates-General, a body of representatives elected from the nobility, the clergy, and the common people. But the commoners of this body—called the Third Estate—wanted more say in the running of the government. They wanted the king to pass social reforms before new taxes. When the king failed to do so, the commoners broke away from the Estates-General and formed a new body, the National Assembly. Spurred on by the Jacobins, a powerful political group that supported the Assembly, people began rebelling throughout the kingdom.

Frenchmen were divided over the Revolution, but Napoleon supported it and the Jacobins. While mob violence waged on in France, Napoleon and the French army fought wars against Austria, Prussia, and England. Because of his great accomplishments on the battlefield, Napoleon was promoted to brigadier general in 1794. The following year he held off an angry mob in Paris that threatened the National Convention, an elected body that was writing a new constitution. The Directory, a group of five men chosen by the Convention to run the government, rewarded Napoleon in 1796 by appointing him commander of the army of Italy.

He left for Italy to fight Austria only a few days after marrying the beautiful Josephine de Beauharnais. His army was poorly trained and supplied. But through his military

genius—he never fought two battles using the same method—it soon became a superior fighting force. By October 1797 Napoleon had defeated the Austrians and had gained Belgium and the west bank of the Rhine River for France. He returned to France a hero. Soon restless, he took troops and scientists to Egypt in 1798, hoping to seize the country and cut off trade routes for England, still at war with France. Initially he was successful, and French scientists found the Rosetta Stone (the key to ancient hieroglyphics) and began the study of Egyptology. But the English soon destroyed the French navy and Napoleon was forced to return to France.

## Becomes Emperor Napoleon I

Napoleon found conditions in France very bad. The Directory was weak and ineffective. The French people were not alarmed, then, when Napoleon and a few others overthrew the Directory and seized control of the government in November of 1799. Napoleon presented France with a new constitution calling for three consuls to rule, each for a period of ten years. Napoleon became the first consul and created a government staffed by talented men, not just nobles. He restored law and order by establishing a strong police force, and he signed peace treaties with Austria and England. Because of these policies, the French voted Napoleon consul for life in 1802. Just two years later, the people agreed to make him emperor of France. He now had unlimited power. At the crowning ceremony, he took the crown from the hands of the pope and placed it on his own head.

But Napoleon was a reformer and lawmaker, and France prospered under his leadership. He created the Bank of France, stabilized the nation's financial system, and forced everyone to pay taxes. Grants were given to new industries and prizes were given out for new inventions. He had new roads built and new crops introduced. He established the Napoleonic codes, laws that regulated social rights like individual liberty, religious freedom, and divorce (with some revision, these codes are still in use today). He also built classical monuments, added great art works to the Louvre museum, and enlarged the national library. Under Napoleon's direction, a high school educational system was introduced that prepared students for college. Little attention, however, was given to the education of women. In Napoleon's eyes, women were not equal to men, and he limited their rights.

Even though Napoleon had signed a treaty with England, he was still determined to invade and defeat this nation. But to do this, Napoleon had to have control over the English Channel. So in October 1805 the French navy battled the English fleet at Trafalgar, a cape on the southwest coast of Spain. Under Admiral Horatio Nelson (who was killed by a sniper during the battle) the English crushed the French, and Napoleon never challenged England at sea again.

## Changes Map of Europe

England feared Napoleon's presence on the European continent and convinced Austria, Russia, and Sweden to join it against him. Napoleon's mighty army, however, defeated the

Austrians at Ulm (present-day southern Germany) and the combined forces of the Austrians and Russians at Austerlitz (present-day, southeast Czech republic) in 1805. The battle of Austerlitz ended this coalition of nations against France, and changed the map of Europe. Austria lost possession of its German and Italian states and with them, the crown of the Holy Roman emperor. In 1806 Napoleon gathered these territories together into the Confederation of the Rhine, and the Holy Roman Empire was no more.

Now master of many lands, Napoleon sought to conquer powerful Prussia, the last stronghold in northern central Europe. He did so within a week. He now appeared unstoppable. Having defeated the great powers of Europe, he dominated the continent from the Atlantic to the borders of Russia. But more than anything, Napoleon wanted to defeat England. Since he could not invade the country, he decided to destroy her economy. In 1806 Napoleon established the Continental System, which forbade European countries from trading with England.

But the System sprang leaks: countries began secretly to open their ports to the English. Napoleon believed Spain was guilty of this and invaded the country in 1807. For five years the Spanish lost every battle they fought with the French, yet they did not lose the war. Their strong resistance inspired Austria to renew its war with France in 1809. Although Napoleon quickly defeated them, his troubles were not over. He and his wife, Josephine, could not bear a son—an heir. Therefore, Napolean reluctantly divorced her in December 1809. The following March he married the 18-year-old Marie Louise of Austria. A son was born one year later.

Napoleon's happiness did not last long. Countries throughout Europe were growing tired of French dominance. People wanted independence and the right to rule their own lands. At the end of 1810 Russia withdrew its support of the Continental System and broke any alliance it had with France. Therefore, in 1812 Napoleon invaded Russia with over 500,000 troops. Greatly outnumbered, the Russians retreated, burning villages and crops along the way. The French could find no food or shelter in this barren land and when winter set in, they suffered. The Russians refused to negotiate and, with-

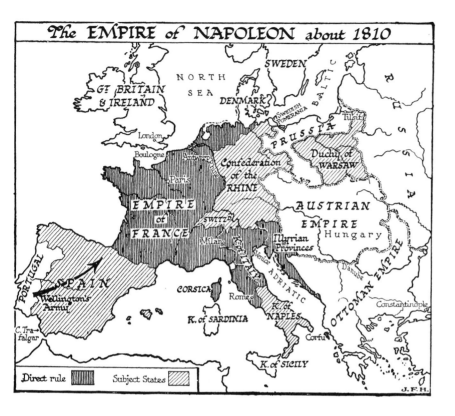

The EMPIRE of NAPOLEON about 1810

Direct rule | Subject States

J.F.H.

out supplies, the French had to retreat. By the time Napoleon reached Vilnius (in present-day Lithuania), only 40,000 of his troops remained.

## Russian Defeat Brings Downfall

Napoleon's Russian campaign was a tremendous defeat. Knowing the French army was weak, European nations banded together and attacked. Napoleon lost battles and soon France was invaded. On March 31, 1814, Paris fell, and Napoleon abdicated (gave up the throne) a few weeks later. Louis XVIII was placed on the French throne, and Napoleon was taken to the island of Elba off the western coast of Italy to live as an outcast the rest of his life. But he had other plans. In March 1815 he escaped from Elba, landed on the French coast, and marched to Paris, gathering support as he went. King Louis XVIII fled and Napoleon reclaimed the crown on March 20, 1815.

Napoleon appealed to the other European countries for peace, but they refused to trust him and warfare began again. In present-day central Belgium, the famous battle of Waterloo was fought. Under the British general Arthur Wellington, the combined British and Prussian forces overwhelmed Napoleon. It was his last battle, and his second period of rule, known as the Hundred Days, came to an end. He surrendered to the British on June 15, asking to live in England. But the British refused his request and took him to the island of Saint Helena in the south Atlantic, 1300 miles off the coast of Africa. Painfully suffering from stomach cancer, Napoleon died there on May 5, 1821. In December 1840 his remains were returned to France and buried in Paris beneath the grand dome of the Invalides.

# Alexander Nevsky

*Prince of Novgorod
and grand prince of Vladimir*

*Born c. 1220*

*Died 1263*

A lexander Nevsky came to power in the thirteenth century as Russia was being invaded and overrun by Mongols, Lithuanians, Swedes, and Teutonic Knights. Had he not been a strong leader with a vision for the future, Russia might have been destroyed. If that had happened, the history of Eastern Europe would have been changed and, quite possibly, also that of the entire world. For his wise leadership through this troubled time, Alexander is honored to this day as a Russian national hero.

In the ninth century, the Varangian (Viking) warrior Rurik conquered the city of Novgorod (in modern northwest Russia) and founded a dynasty. His relative and successor, Oleg, moved south and captured the city of Kiev (in modern Ukraine), establishing a new state there. Varangians were also known as Rus or Rhos. So as this new state grew from its center in Kiev, it became known as Kievan Russia (Kievan Rus). In the eleventh century, Kievan Russia extended from the Baltic Sea in the north to the Black Sea in the south. The land

*"By swallowing his pride as a ruler, Alexander saved the lives of his people."*

it occupied included almost all of modern Ukraine, Belarus, and northwest Russia.

Just before Yaroslav the Wise, grand prince of Kiev, died in 1154, he divided Kievan Russia into principalities, each to be ruled by his sons as princes. However, they still were to obey the rule of the grand prince in Kiev. But they did not, and soon declared independence in their own realms. Civil wars developed. By the middle of the twelfth century, power was no longer centered in Kiev in the south, but spread out over the principalities. Chief among these was Vladimir-Suzdal in the northwest. But with no central power, these divided principalities were open to attacks from invaders. And the people who took advantage of this were the Mongols.

## Fierce Mongols Invade Russia

The Mongols were nomadic (wandering) tribes of people who lived in the area north of China. Early in the thirteenth century these tribes were united under a ruler known to history as Genghis Khan (see **Genghis Khan**). Under his leadership the Mongols conquered China, then moved west to defeat the Kipchak Turks (known to the Russians as Polovetsians), nomadic tribes living on the steppes or plains along the Black Sea. The Mongols were extremely fierce fighters. They were often victorious because of their sheer number, sending wave after wave of attackers to wear down their enemies. If enemies surrendered, their lives and property were spared. If they did not, the Mongols destroyed their city and killed every man, woman, and child. They even burned the crops and slaughtered the cattle. Genghis Khan died in 1227. His grandson Batu then led the Mongols in their invasion and destruction of Kievan Russia beginning in 1237.

Alexander had been born around 1220, shortly before the first Mongol raids against the Kipchak Turks. His father, Yaroslav II, became grand prince of Vladimir in 1236. Yaroslav then made his son prince of Novgorod, now a principality in the north. But with the Mongol raids in 1237, Kievan Russia came to an end. Among others, the cities of Vladimir, Moscow, and Kiev fell. Many princes were killed trying to defend their realms. By 1240, the Mongols controlled most of Russia. Batu Khan then founded the city of Sarai on the lower Volga River just north of its entry into the Caspian Sea. It soon became the capital of the Mongol empire in Russia. Because of the magnificent tent camp that Batu set up at Satai and because of the wealth acquired by the Mongols, their empire came to be known as the "Golden Horde."

Because the Mongol invasion weakened what remained of Russia, the western neighbors sought to claim what they could. In 1240 the Swedes tried to capture the Neva River and Lake Ladoga, just to the north of Novgorod. But Alexander met them on the banks of the Neva with a small force and quickly defeated them. Thereafter, he was known as Alexander Nevsky—Russian for "of the Neva." His battles, though, were not over. The Teutonic Knights, a German military religious order, took the city of Pskov, southwest of Novgorod. In 1242 Alexander and his brother Andrew fought the Knights on the frozen surface of nearby Lake Peipus. In this "Battle on the Ice," hundreds of Germans were killed. Others died by falling through the ice into the freezing waters.

Two years later, Alexander drove off Lithuanian raiders, defeating them twice with only a small force.

## Alexander Cooperates with Mongols

In the meantime, the Mongols controlled Russia by a simple rule: they owned everything and had the power of life and death over everyone. But they allowed Russian princes to continue governing in their principalities as long as they paid tribute (taxes) to the Mongols. Alexander cooperated with the Mongols. He realized they were less of a threat to Russia than the enemies in the West, who wanted to convert the Orthodox Russians to Catholicism. For this, many of his fellow Russians thought he was a traitor. But by swallowing his pride as a ruler, Alexander saved the lives of his people.

In 1252 the Mongol leaders made Alexander the grand prince of Vladimir (his father had been poisoned to death six years earlier). Once again, he had to protect the Russian people against attacks by the Germans, the Swedes, and the

Lithuanians. He was successful on all fronts. Throughout his reign, Alexander used his influence at Sarai to help ease the Mongol rule over the Russian people. In 1263, returning from his fourth trip to Sarai to negotiate with the Mongol leaders, Alexander died.

Alexander was a savior of Russia from it enemies in the East and the West. He was a brilliant and undefeated military commander. And as a ruler, he was wise and farsighted. He knew the Russian people would outlast the Mongol empire. He was right: the empire broke up in the fourteenth century. The Russian people, forever grateful, made Alexander a saint in the Orthodox Church in 1547. And in 1725, to further honor his name, Russian empress Catherine I founded the Order of Alexander Nevsky, a high-ranking military order.

# Otto I, the Great

*German king,*
*founder of Holy Roman Empire*
*Born October 23, 912*
*Died May 7, 973*

A t the beginning of the tenth century, the territory that now makes up modern Germany was still wild. Dense forests covered the land, broken only here and there by open fields surrounding small settlements or villages. Occasionally a tower from an abbey or a church rose among the tall trees. This untouched land had once been under the control of the Frank king Charlemagne (see **Charlemagne**). His great empire spread across Europe in the eighth and ninth centuries. But less than 50 years after his death, his grandsons signed the Treaty of Verdun that split his empire into three kingdoms. One of these covered this thick forestland.

This area was divided into duchies, or territories ruled by dukes. The five greatest of these were Franconia, Saxony, Thuringia, Swabia, and Bavaria. Traditionally, a king ruled over these duchies. But by 912, the year of Otto's birth, the dukes had become very powerful. They considered themselves equal to the king who ruled over them. And they gave their support to him only if he gave them something in return. The

*"Otto's empire—known as the Holy Roman Empire a few centuries later—would be the empire known to the Middle Ages."*

German people would not be united under a single ruler until Otto became king. His raising of the kingship to a position of power over these duchies became his first great achievement. His second achievement was the expansion of this kingdom into a domain that became known as the Holy Roman Empire. Stretching over Europe in various forms, this empire lasted for almost 900 years.

Otto was the eldest son of Matilda and Henry I, the duke of Saxony who was later elected king over the duchies. Growing up like most early medieval nobles, Otto learned how to hunt, to ride horses, and to fight in battle. But he never received a formal education, a trait he shared with most kings of his time. He learned to read, as did Charlemagne, only after he became king. In 929 he wed Edith, an Anglo-Saxon princess who was the sister of King Athelstan of England.

When Henry I died in 936, the dukes and nobles of the realm elected Otto king. They all promised to support him. But Otto's reign began uneasily. First, outside enemies raided the borders of his kingdom. Chief among his attackers were the Magyars, invaders originally from the Ural Mountains region in modern west-central Russia. Like the Huns, they were nomads (wanderers), fierce fighters, and excellent horsemen. Otto defeated these enemies, but he would come to face them again. Otto's kingdom was threatened then from the inside. Three dukes and members of his own family, including his half-brother Thankmar and his full brother Henry, rose up against Otto's rule. But he put down these rebellions. And by 947, to ensure that his kingdom was secure, Otto had given command of the duchies to trustworthy members of his family. Full peace in his kingdom, however, was yet to come.

## Wants to Rule an Empire

Otto's main desire was to rule an empire much like that of Charlemagne's. He was given the chance to achieve this beginning in 951. The widowed Italian queen Adelaide was being forced into a marriage with the son of Berengar II, count of Ivrea, who wanted the Italian throne for himself. She appealed to Otto for help. Otto led his army into Italy and rescued Adelaide, marrying her shortly afterward (his first wife had died in 946). Taking the title of King of Italy, he wanted to become Roman emperor but was forced to return to Germany.

New attacks on his kingdom, both from within and from without, awaited Otto. His eldest son by his first marriage, Liudolf, raised a revolt against him. Although the resulting battles were brutal, Otto crushed those who opposed him. In the end, though, Otto was merciful, pardoning Luidolf when he begged for his father's forgiveness. But no sooner had this conflict ended then Otto was forced to meet the Magyars again. In August of 955 he led his troops against them at Lechfeld, a plain in what is now southern Germany. Otto acted swiftly and courageously, and his victory was complete. The Magyars fled, never to return.

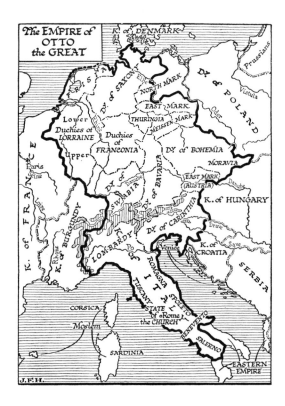

## Receives Emperor's Crown

Meanwhile, in Italy, Berengar had taken over, ruling like a tyrant. Pope John XII pleaded with Otto to help remove him. Otto soon marched his awesome army into Italy. And on February 2, 962, in the cathedral of St. Peter in Rome, the pope crowned Otto and Adelaide emperor and empress of Rome. Otto's ambition had been fulfilled. He became the most powerful ruler in the West. His empire was not as big as Charlemagne's—it included only the German duchies, northern Italy, and Burgundy (area in modern southeast France). But his empire—known as the Holy Roman Empire a few centuries later—would be *the* empire known to the Middle Ages. And it would not come to an end until the beginning of the nineteenth century.

Otto's problems did not end with his coronation, though. The pope soon believed Otto's rule was too strong, and negotiated with Otto's enemies. Upon learning this, Otto returned to Rome and removed John XII, making Leo VIII the new pope. Otto's actions—taking the title of emperor and installing a new pope—upset the Byzantine Empire in Constantinople (what was left of the former Roman Empire). Over the next six years, battles were fought between the two empires over the control of southern Italy. A peace settlement finally was reached in 972, calling for the marriage of the Byzantine princess Theophano to Otto's son and successor, Otto II. His work completed in Italy, Otto returned to Germany. He died the following year, having ruled as king for 37 years and as emperor for 11.

# Saint Patrick

*Patron saint of Ireland*
*Born c. 395*
*Died c. 460*

St. Patrick's Day, March 17, is observed by Catholics and non-Catholics alike. The occasion is often marked by cheerful, light-hearted celebrations. But the story of the historical Patrick has little in common with this day of merriment. Patrick, who converted the Irish people to Christianity in the first century A.D., is an example of a simple history being changed into a fanciful and colorful fiction. Perhaps the most reliable source of information about him is his own writing—the *Confessions*. It is one of only two Latin texts written outside the boundaries of the Roman Empire that have survived from that time.

Patrick wrote his *Confessions* when he was an old man. He composed this work as a long response to clear his name from charges that as a young man he committed a grave sin. Patrick did not intend it to be an autobiography, but it does cover his entire life. According to the *Confessions,* he was born in England. The actual date of his birth is unknown, but it probably fell sometime during the last years that Rome controlled

*"Patrick was successful in his mission because he understood the country and its people and converted them tribe by tribe."*

Britain (the Empire's collapse there began in 409). He was the son of Calpurnius, a minor Roman noblemen, and the grandson of the priest Potitus. Despite coming from such a noble family, Patrick received a very poor education (his later writings were composed in a strange mix of classical and common Latin).

## Sold Into Slavery by Pirates

At the age of 16, Patrick was captured by pirates and carried across the Irish Sea to be sold as a slave in Ireland. Although he was raised a Catholic, he became especially religious during his years of enslavement. "My spirit was moved," he wrote, "so that in a single day I would say as many as a hundred prayers, and almost as many at night." Patrick believed he had been captured because he had not been faithful in his worship of God.

After six years of slavery as a shepherd, Patrick had a dream urging him to escape and to return home. He later wrote in the *Confessions* that he had to cover "two hundred miles" to get to the coast of Ireland. Then he had to convince a group of sailors to take him on board their ship. He eventually returned home, but his dreams once again forced him to act. This time Patrick dreamed he was "visited by a man named Victorius" who told him to return to Ireland and convert its people to Christianity. Around 419 he left his homeland to study for the priesthood, possible at Auxerre, France, under the guidance of Saint Germain. There he remained for the next 12 years before heading to Ireland.

Although he is the patron saint of Ireland, Patrick was not the first to preach there. The bishop Palladius went there in 431, but failed as a missionary (a person who tries to convert others to different religious beliefs). He left the country after a year and died on the way home. Patrick then became the second missionary bishop sent to Ireland when he traveled there the following year.

Patrick's preachings, however, were much more widespread than Palladius's. In the Roman Empire at that time, Christianity was practiced mainly in the cities. But Patrick daringly took it to the countryside, and even beyond the borders of the Empire. By his own account, he converted and baptized hundreds of Irish men and women. His mission, though, was not without danger. Many non-Christians, especially local kings and authorities, were hostile to Patrick's teachings. Many times his life was threatened; one time he was jailed for two weeks.

## Truth or Just Legends?

Beyond these descriptions, it is hard to know the truth about Patrick's work. Through the years historians have colored his life with legendary and miraculous tales. For instance, according to legend, Patrick used the clover leaf to explain the Holy Trinity to an Irish king (that is why it has since become his symbol). Another legend states that Patrick drove all the snakes out of Ireland. He also supposedly brought on earthquakes, sudden darkness, and general confusion to areas where people refused to convert. And in one wild tale, Patrick had a wizard, who mocked both God and him, lifted high into the air and then dropped to the ground, where he smashed to pieces.

In reality, Patrick was successful in his mission because he understood the country and its people and converted them tribe by tribe. As Bishop of the Irish, he helped organize and change Irish laws. He softened especially those laws concerning slaves and the taxation of the poor. At the time of his death, Ireland was almost entirely Christian. This has made Patrick one of the most successful missionaries in history.

# Robert I, the Bruce

*King of Scots*

*Born July 11, 1274,*
*Turnberry Castle, Scotland*

*Died June 7, 1329,*
*Cardross, Scotland*

*"Robert set the country free from English rule, bringing independence to Scotland that lasted for almost three centuries."*

Scotland in the thirteenth century occupied about the same territory that it does today. Within this compact land lived an assortment of peoples. The people living in the Highlands and the western islands were strongly Gaelic, recalling their Norse (Viking) ancestry. Those in Lothian, in the south, were of Anglo-Saxon (English) descent. Elsewhere, French heritage was spread by Anglo-Norman aristocrats who settled in Scotland during the two centuries after the Norman duke William conquered England (see **William the Conqueror**) in 1066. All these people of different racial backgrounds were united by a strong kingship and by the idea that they were all free members of a Scottish community.

This Scottish identity, however, was threatened in March 1286 when King Alexander III fell from his horse on a dark, rainy night and broke his neck. England then gained control of Scotland and would not release its hold. Civil wars erupted. One man finally came forward to end these battles and to restore the Scottish monarchy. His name was Robert, of the

Bruce family. He set the country free from English rule, bringing independence to Scotland that lasted for almost three centuries.

Robert was born on July 11, 1274 at Turnberry Castle, the remains of which can still be seen perched on a cliff overlooking the Firth of Clyde in southeast Scotland. He was the eldest son of Marjorie and Robert, the earl of Carrick. As the son of a nobleman, Robert received an education that focused on military skills and horsemanship. He probably also learned to speak all the languages of his countrymen—English, French, and Gaelic. When Robert was 18 years old, his father resigned the earldom of Carrick and gave it to him.

## Scots Come Under English Rule

The Bruces were an important Anglo-Norman family with ties to previous Scottish kings. When King Alexander died, followed by his young daughter shortly afterward, the Scottish kingship was open. Over a dozen men then claimed the throne, including Robert's grandfather. Acting as judge, King Edward I of England decided in November 1292 that John Balliol was the new king of Scotland. Over the next few years, however, tensions developed between England and Scotland, and in 1296 Edward forced John and Scottish nobles (including the Bruces) to submit to him. The government of Scotland then came under English control.

This rule soon sparked uprisings. The leader of the resistance was William Wallace, who defeated the English at the battle of Stirling Bridge in September of 1297, but was overwhelmed by the enemy forces the following July. Wallace then resigned as leader, and the position went to both Robert and John Comyn, who was related to John Balliol's family through marriage. Because the Bruces and the Balliols were old rivals, however, Robert refused to share the leadership with Comyn and resigned in 1300. Two years later, he switched his allegiance to King Edward, even marrying Elizabeth de Burgh, an Irish earl's daughter who supported Edward.

An event soon changed the course of Robert's life. For unknown reasons, he met Comyn in February 1306 at a Franciscan church in Dumfries in southern Scotland. The meeting ended in a quarrel, and Comyn was killed by Robert and his companions. The murder was not planned, but it seemed Robert wanted the Scottish throne all along. Defying Edward, Robert was crowned king of Scotland in March 1306. But Edward was quick to attack, defeating the Scottish forces twice that summer. Many of Robert's supporters were captured and three of his brothers were killed. Robert soon disappeared.

## Learns Courage From Watching Spider

Legend states that Robert hid in a cave where, watching a spider trying to spin a web over and over, he learned to have hope and courage. Whatever the case, he returned to Scotland in January 1307 and was finally victorious in battle. While attempting to lead a new attack against him in July, Edward died. His son and heir, Edward II, was a poor soldier and king, and by 1309 Robert had recaptured two-thirds of Scotland. Even though he established his rule throughout northern Scotland over the next four years, the English still had strongholds in the south. But one by one these soon fell to the Scottish, the final battle taking place in June 1314. On the moor (swampy wasteland) of Bannockburn in south-central Scotland, Robert and his ragged army soundly defeated the large English force. After this victory, all of Scotland hailed Robert as king, thus ending any remaining conflicts between countrymen.

Robert's kingship was not recognized by Edward, and for almost the next ten years raids and battles continued. Finally, in 1323, Edward II and Robert signed a truce, though it made no mention of Robert as the rightful king of Scotland. When Edward III took over the English throne from his father in 1327 he led an army against Scotland. He was unsuccessful and was forced in 1328 to sign the Treaty of Northampton. It not only recognized Robert's kingship but also Scotland's independence. Robert's 20-year struggle against England was over: his country was free.

By the time the treaty was signed, Robert's health was failing. He soon retired to his castle in Cardross in southeast Scotland where he died on June 7, 1329, perhaps of leprosy.

The Scottish kingship then went to his son David. According to Robert's wishes, his heart was to be removed, embalmed, and carried by Sir James Douglas (a Scottish nobleman) to Jerusalem, then buried. Douglas never made it to Jerusalem though; he was killed in battle against the Muslims in Spain. Robert's heart, however, was recovered, returned to Scotland, and reportedly buried in Melrose Abbey.

# Rudolf I, of Habsburg

*First Habsburg king of Germany*
*Born 1218*
*Died 1291*

*"Through his dealings, Rudolf established political power in Austria that his family maintained until 1918, a span of almost 700 years."*

I n Rudolf I's time, most rulers came to power early in their lives, some even before the age of 20. When Rudolf became king of the Germans and Holy Roman emperor, he was 55 years old. Previously, he had been a count in the German duchy (territory ruled by a duke) of Swabia. He spent most of his early life as a soldier, but showed signs of being a reasonable and compassionate man. These traits truly emerged when he took the German crown. Most rulers added territory to their kingdoms through battles and conquests. Rudolf secured lands through negotiations and marriages. He was the first member of his family line—Habsburg—to achieve kingship. And he made sure he was not the last. Through his dealings, he established political power in Austria that his family maintained until 1918, a span of almost 700 years.

The Habsburg family can be traced back to the tenth century. They originally held lands in northwest Switzerland and in Alsace, a region in present-day northeast France. The family name came from the castle of Habichts-burg (translated as

"Hawk's Castle") in the Swiss canton (state) of Aargau, just west of the city of Zurich. By the time Rudolf was born in 1218, the Habsburgs had added more estates to their holdings, but they were nothing more than minor German princes.

## Elected German King

In 1254 the German king Conrad IV of the Hohenstaufen family (see **Frederick I (Barbarossa)**), died before securing the throne for this son. The German kingdom was without a king for the next 19 years, a period that came to be known as the "Great Interregnum." Finally, in 1273, the German nobility elected Rudolf the new king. They did so for two reasons: they wanted someone who would not become too powerful and upset their own political control, and they wanted to exclude a rival non-German candidate—Ottokar II.

Rudolf obeyed the wishes of the electors. Since there was no recognized Holy Roman emperor during the interregnum, the control previous emperors had over Italian lands weakened. Rudolf did not try to reclaim this control and build up his power. Instead, he abandoned claims to lands in the southern part of Italy and to the Papal States—lands in central Italy governed by the pope. Although Rudolf was recognized by Pope Gregory X as the new emperor, he was never officially crowned. (Because of this, his oldest son, Albert, did not inherit the title of emperor after Rudolf's death.)

Meanwhile, Ottokar rose against the German nobility. He was the powerful king of Bohemia, a former kingdom that in 1918 became part of Czechoslovakia (present-day Czech Republic). He claimed that he was an elector, but had not voted. So he refused to recognize Rudolf as the new king. The other electors banned together and stripped Ottakar of all the lands he controlled outside of Bohemia. In a clever political move, Rudolf convinced Austrian nobility who had been friends with Ottokar to join with him. Without any warfare, Ottokar was forced to surrender his claims to Carinthia, Styria, and Carniola—regions making up the Austrian state.

## Founds Dynasty in Austria

Just a few years later, however, Ottokar believed Rudolf was not as powerful as he once appeared to be. Ottokar, therefore, tried to reclaim the lands that had been taken away from him. This meant war. In 1278 Rudolf united his forces and led them across the March River, which lay between Austria and Bohemia. Near the town of Durnkraut, Rudolf's army overwhelmed the Bohemians. Ottokar was killed. Rudolf then acquired the lands Ottokar controlled, and placed them in the hands of his sons Albrecht and Rudolf. These Austrian lands became the center of the Habsburg dynasty that ruled until 1918.

The battle against Ottokar was the last one Rudolf had to fight. A rough and heroic military commander early in his life, he became a near-saintly king and emperor. After his crowning, he forgave all those who had harmed him and released those he had imprisoned. Cooperating with the German nobility, he made great efforts to enforce the public peace in Germany. His taxation of the areas he controlled, however, led to some resistance. At his death in 1291, three Swiss cantons united to form their own alliance. This was the beginning of the Swiss Confederacy, also known as the country of Switzerland. The lasting effect of Rudolf's reign, however, was the continuation of his family's position in Europe through marriages to other royal houses. Many of his descendants became important rulers in Europe, including the Spanish king and Holy Roman emperor Charles V (see **Charles V**).

# Stephen I

*First king of Hungary*
*Born c. 973*
*Died 1038*

The founders of the modern country of Hungary were the Magyars. They originally came from the region between the Volga River and the Ural Mountains in what is now west-central Russia. The Magyars were nomads (wanderers), constantly forced to move by other advancing tribes. But they were also ferocious warriors and trained horsemen. As they moved across central Europe in the first half of the tenth century, they spread terror. But their history and their way of life suddenly changed in August 955. They suffered a crushing defeat at the hands of the German king Otto I (see **Otto I, the Great**). The Magyars, under the rule of Taksony, returned to the land they had already conquered (site of modern Hungary) and settled there for good.

Taksony's son, the duke Géza, took over in 972. He tried to create a sense of order in his tribe and to develop political ties to western European countries. He even had his son, Stephen, marry the German princess Gisela, daughter of the duke of Bavaria. To unite the Magyars/Hungarians, he turned

*"He had founded the Hungarian nation and, through his fair and diplomatic rule, it grew and lasted."*

to Christianity. But many of the nobles in his tribe opposed him and continued to follow their own religious beliefs. When Géza died in 997 and Stephen became chief, he was faced with the same opposition.

## Founds Christian Kingdom of Hungary

Stephen, however, sensed that more direct action was needed. So three years later he asked Pope Sylvester II to baptize him and to crown him king of Hungary. Because the pope recognized Stephen as a Christian ruler, it reduced the possibility that the Holy Roman Empire would take over his kingdom. Hungary thus remained free. The crown that the pope sent to Stephen has remained to this day a sacred symbol of Hungary's independent existence. But as the crown was being sent from Rome to Hungary, it was damaged. When it was placed on Stephen's head on Christmas Day of 1000, the cross on top was bent. That defect, too, has remained to this day.

As king, Stephen was faced with great problems. One of these was the revolt of his cousin Koppàny who ruled in Transylvania. (The Magyars had entered this historic region in what is now central Romania in the fifth century.) Koppàny claimed the throne of Hungary as his. He also claimed Stephen's widowed mother as his wife. Stephen immediately moved against him. Two years later, he defeated Koppàny and executed him. Another Magyar then claimed the rule in Transylvania, but Stephen quickly defeated him and made Transylvania part of his Hungarian kingdom in 1003.

Like the great Frankish king Charlemagne (see **Charlemagne**), Stephen vigorously tried to spread Christianity throughout his realm. He established schools and churches. And he encouraged the nobility to fund the building and the running of monasteries. Some historians have reported that, like Charlemagne, Stephen was not afraid to use force to convert his people to Christianity. But he also accepted other religious practices when necessary. To help the economy grow, he invited Jewish and Muslim traders into his kingdom, but he ordered a strict toleration of their religious practices.

# Wins Respect Inside/Outside Kingdom

Whether he was too forceful in Christianizing his people, Stephen did design laws for his new kingdom that helped them. He had formed his kingdom like other European monarchies, but his laws differed slightly. They were Christianized versions of Magyar customs and traditions. While the laws did bring order to his kingdom, they also met the needs of his people. He also divided his kingdom into counties governed by officials. This prevented the nobility in Hungary from abusing their power. His development of this fair-minded social structure won him the respect of people throughout his realm.

Stephen also established good relations with those outside his kingdom. He helped Byzantine emperor Basil II in his battle with the Bulgarians. When the Byzantines were victorious, Stephen was able to establish both trade and religious connections with the Empire. But he also had been humane and considerate to Bulgarian prisoners. And because of this, the Hungarian and Bulgarian kingdoms were able to peacefully overcome any differences that remained. Stephen's good relationships with neighboring kingdoms soon proved valuable. In 1030 the German emperor Conrad II attacked the western parts of Hungary. Since Stephen did not have to worry about attacks on his other borders, he used all his forces against the Germans. They were defeated and withdrew.

But Stephen suffered tragedies in his personal life. Although he ruled successfully for almost 40 years, he was not able to pass on his crown to his family. His only son, Imre, died in what some believe was a hunting accident (killed by a "wild boar"). But others believe Imre was assassinated by a powerful Hungarian family that did not want to convert to Christianity. In either case, Imre had been well-loved by the Christian Hungarians because he had led a life of virtue and courage. The Hungarians canonized him (declared him to be a saint) in the late eleventh century. Stephen was also canonized about the same time. He had founded the Hungarian nation and, through his fair and diplomatic rule, it grew and lasted. For this, Stephen is known as the patron saint of Hungary.

# Victoria

*English queen*
*May 24, 1819,*
*Kensington Palace, London, England*
*Died January 22, 1901,*
*Osborne House, Isle of Wight*

*"Even though the power of Victoria's throne weakened, her dignity and high sense of duty made the monarchy more popular and ensured its existence."*

In the nineteenth century, many British explorers set off for adventure and discovery on behalf of their beloved queen, Victoria. Because of this, many places throughout the world are named for her. The largest lake in Africa is Victoria Lake. The most populated state in Australia is Victoria. In Canada, the capital of British Columbia and an island in the Northwest Territories bear her name. And in Antarctica, a large region is known as Victoria Land. She wore the English crown longer than anyone in history. When she became queen in 1837 the monarchy in England was in danger. Control of the government was shifting to Parliament, the legislative body of England. Even though the power of her throne weakened, her dignity and high sense of duty made the monarchy more popular and ensured its existence.

Victoria was the daughter of Duke Edward of Kent (son of King George III) and Princess Mary Louisa Victoria of Saxe-Coburg-Saalfeld in Germany. Victoria was eight months old when her father died, and only two childless uncles stood between her and the throne. Her mother and her mother's majordomo (head steward) then invented a system to make Victoria their puppet, so that when she became queen they would actually rule the land. Growing up, Victoria had to sleep in her mother's room every night. She could not see anyone without her mother or the majordomo present, and she could not go anywhere alone. She even had to keep a diary, which her mother read every morning to know what she was thinking.

Victoria became queen a month after her eighteenth birthday when her last uncle died. She immediately took control of her life, banishing her mother to another part of the royal palace. But Victoria had not been properly educated for the throne, and for advice she relied on her prime minister, William Melbourne. He quickly became for Victoria the father she never had. Under his guidance, Victoria learned about England's history and the function of its monarch. Although she had limited power, Victoria demanded to know the daily workings of the government and gave her opinion on it.

## Marriage Changes Life

Victoria's life was permanently changed in 1840 when she married her first cousin Prince Albert of Saxe-Coburg-Gotha. Very much in love, Victoria soon became extremely happy as a wife and mother, giving birth to nine children. Many of them married into other royal families in Europe, including those in Russia, Germany, and Denmark. The kings Carl XVI Gustaf of Sweden and Juan Carlos I of Spain are direct descendants of Victoria. Because of these family connections, she became known as the Grandmother of Europe.

Albert was an extremely intelligent man, and his influence on Victoria was great. He was a stickler for manners and hard work, and Victoria soon adopted these traits. He also moderated her political thinking. Previously, Victoria was loyal to Melbourne and his Whig Party. When the Tory Party and its leader, Robert Peel, came to power in 1841, Albert persuaded Victoria to accept them. Thus began the practice of the English monarch being politically neutral and able to work with whatever party controlled Parliament. Albert also con-

*Victoria meeting with her advisors*

vinced Victoria to support the arts and sciences. The famous Crystal Palace (made of iron, glass, and wood), the Victoria and Albert Museum, and the Royal Albert Hall were all built during her reign.

At the beginning of the 1850s, Victoria was extremely popular. But this popularity began to disappear with the outbreak of the Crimean War in 1853. With the decline of the

Ottoman Empire, Russia sought control over the eastern Mediterranean. England, France, and Sardinia (an island in the western Mediterranean) soon joined forces against Russia. Initially, many people believed Victoria and Albert sided with the Russians. Victoria proved this belief false by helping organize relief efforts for the wounded and by creating the Victoria Cross, a medal given for bravery in battle.

The first half of Victoria's life ended when Albert died from typhoid fever on December 14, 1861. The queen was devastated and suffered a nervous breakdown. She never got over the loss of her husband, and had his clothes laid out on their bed every night for the rest of her life. She did not appear in public for almost three years. Her most-favored politician, Benjamin Disraeli, finally convinced her to return to her public duties. He then became the third man to have a great influence over the queen's life.

## Pushes for English Imperialism

The older Victoria grew, the more she adopted Disraeli's conservative approach to government. Even though the prime minister William Ewart Gladstone opposed imperialism (the act of taking control over another country mostly for economic reasons), Disraeli and Victoria favored it. England's imperial power soon spread over many regions in Africa and into Iran, Afghanistan, and China. When Disraeli made her empress of India in 1876, the queen was greatly pleased.

To further her country's imperialism, Victoria eagerly supported the South African War (also known as the Boer War). Begun in 1899, this conflict pitted the English against the Boers (Dutch descendants living in Africa) for control over Transvaal and the Orange Free State, areas in the present-day Republic of South Africa. She died in 1901 before the war was over (England emerged the victor a year later). To the end Victoria maintained her dignified manner, and this made her immensely popular with the English people. Her son, Edward VII, succeeded her to the throne.

# William the Conqueror

*Duke of Normandy and king of England*
*Born c. 1027*
*Died September 9, 1087*

*"William changed the course of the history of England."*

Many historians consider 1066 to be one of the most important dates in European history. In that year the Norman duke William defeated the English king Harold at the battle of Hastings. He then became known as William the Conqueror, the new English king, and changed the course of the history of England. He did so by introducing *feudalism* as a means of governing. Although feudalism already existed in England, William's system increased the power of the throne. Almost the entire kingdom became the property of the king, and he ruled supreme.

William was born around 1027 in Normandy, a region in northwest France bordering the English Channel. Over 100 years before, Vikings—called Norsemen or Northmen—raided France and attacked the cities of Paris and Chartres. The Norse chief Rollo then signed a treaty with the French king Charles III, and gained control of the territory he and his men had already conquered. That area came to be known as Normandy, and Rollo became its first duke. Over time, marriages between the Norsemen and the French natives living in Normandy produced a thoroughly blended society of people, the Normans.

William was the son of Herleve and the Norman duke Robert I, a direct descendent of Rollo. Because his parents were not married, he was called William the Bastard. Although relationships like that of his parents were common in the eleventh century, William was not easily embraced by the upper classes in his society. Robert had a difficult time convincing the nobility to accept his illegitimate son as his successor. Finally they relented. When Robert died on the way home from a journey to Jerusalem in 1035, William became duke. But he was only eight years old, and chaos soon spread through Normandy.

## William Is Knighted

Even though the two guardians appointed to protect the young duke suffered violent deaths, William escaped harm. He was knighted when he turned 15 and was determined to stop his rebellious nobles. He sought the aid of the French king Henry I. In an important battle in 1047, the king himself helped William to victory. William returned the favor in 1051 by helping the king defeat Geoffrey Martel, the powerful count of Anjou, a region in northwest France.

Both battles demonstrated William's bravery and skill as a warrior. But he could also be ferocious, as he proved to the citizens of the Norman town of Alencon, who had supported and housed Martel. When William came to fight him, the townspeople hung animal hides from the town walls—a slur against William's mother, whose father was a tanner (person who works hides into leather). To avenge his mother's honor, William brutally attacked the town and mutilated many of its prominent citizens. His power in Normandy was unquestioned after this.

In the early 1050s, William married Matilda, the daughter of the influential count Baldwin V of Flanders, a country immediately east of Normandy. Even though Baldwin was an ally of Henry I, the French king soon turned against William:

he believed the Norman duke was becoming too powerful. When both Henry I and Martel died in 1060, William conquered Maine, a region bordering Normandy and Anjou. His control of Normandy and Maine and his good relationship with the Church established William as a power in Western Europe. It soon led to his Norman Conquest of England.

## Norman Conquest Begins

In January 1066, English king Edward the Confessor died. The English witan (council) then elected Harold Godwineson king. But William, who was the cousin of Edward, thought he was the rightful heir and planned on taking the throne by force. On October 14, 1066, outside the southern England town of Hastings, he led his army of about 7,000 men into battle. The English army, worn out from recent fighting in the north, was crushed and Harold was killed. William marched unopposed to London and was crowned king of England in Westminster Abbey on Christmas Day.

Almost continuous rebellions by English nobles, however, challenged William's power, and he was not able to secure his position until almost 1072. He used these rebellions to his advantage by establishing a strict form of feudalism. This intricate kind of private government existed during the Middle Ages in Western Europe after the reign of the Frank king Charlemagne (see **Charlemagne**).

As strong kings faded, powerful nobles soon held more rights and privileges. They put people under their own rule by having them swear allegiance (fealty). In exchange for this fealty, nobles granted people a piece of land or an estate. This grant was called a fief. The noble who gave the fief was called a suzerain or overlord, and the person to whom it was given was called a vassal. The suzerain settled disputes between vassals and he protected them if they were attacked. Vassals had to pay their suzerain taxes and serve in his military when told. Kings were supposed to have rule over the nobles and the people. But the nobles were the ones who controlled the people; kings often were just figureheads.

Feudalism was fading to some degree in England, but William's form differed significantly. He claimed that all nobles who rebelled against him forfeited their lands, which now belonged to him. He then gave out pieces of these lands (fiefs) to nobles and others who were loyal. William, in a sense, became suzerain over most of the kingdom. This forever altered the landholding patterns of England's nobility.

In order to know his kingdom's resources and to levy taxes, William ordered a census or survey of England in 1085. This invaluable social record, called the *Domesday Book,* was the first of its kind in Europe. In 1086 William also ordered the Oath of Salisbury. This oath guaranteed that people's loyalty to the king was more important than to any of the nobles who owned land and gave out fiefs. Since many of England's nobility had been killed during the conquest in 1066, William had placed many Norman nobles in high positions. This move also helped maintain loyalty in his kingdom.

One result of William's conquest of England that he did not plan on was the creation of the English language. William, members of his court, and most nobles throughout England spoke Norman French. The rest of the people in the kingdom spoke Anglo-Saxon. Over the course of many years, these two languages merged into what is now called Middle English. Modern English—today's language—came directly from this.

Even though his kingdom was secure on the inside, William had to defend it from outside attacks until his death. In 1087, during one of his campaigns of defense, he injured his stomach on the pommel of his saddle while riding his horse. The injury proved fatal, and on September 9, 1089, William the Conqueror died. His second son, William Rufus, then became king of England while his eldest son, Robert, became duke of Normandy.

# Picture Credits

Photographs and illustrations appearing in *World Leaders: People Who Shaped the World* were received from the following sources:

**Courtesy of Chester Beatty Library, Dublin:** volume 1: p. 4; **courtesy of Chinese Information Service:** volume 1: p. 14; **AP/Wide World Photos:** volume 1: pp. 37, 99; **courtesy of the USSR State Archival Fund:** volume 2: p. 256; **courtesy of Caisse Nationale des Monuments Historiques et des Sites, Paris:** volume 2: p. 260; **courtesy of the Organization of American States:** timeline; volume 3: pp. 342, 471, 496; **courtesy of the John F. Kennedy Library,** photo no. AR6283A: timeline; volume 3: p. 391; **courtesy of Franklin D. Roosevelt Library:** volume 3: pp. 442, 447.

# Master Index

*Boldface indicates profile*

Castro, Fidel 380–382, 393

**Catherine II, the Great** 61, **180–183,** 220

Central Intelligence Agency (CIA) 381, 394

Chacabuco, battle of 454

**Champlain, Samuel de 350–352**

Chancellorsville, battle of 408

*Chanson de Roland* (Song of Roland) 187

**Charlemagne** 61, 63, 162, 164, 184, 185, 187, 188, **293–295,** 308, 316

**Charles V** 123, **189–192,** 243, 306, 430

Charles VII 249, 250

Charter of 1611 230

Chattanooga, battle of 378

Chernenko, Konstantin 223

Chernobyl 223

Cheyenne 359, 455, 457

Chi Dao 109

**Chiang Kai–shek 14–17,** 79

**Chief Joseph 353–356**

Chou dynasty 21, 76

**Churchill, Winston 193–196,** 451

Civil rights 366, 369, 392, 395, 396, 398, 399, 417, 419, 446, 483

Civil Rights Act of 1964 399

Civil War, American 335, 336, 340, 358, 364, 367, 375, 376, 378, 407–409, 412, 414, 463, 477–479, 481, 483

Civilian Conservation Corps 450

**Cleopatra VII 18–20,** 106, 169, 174

Cleveland, Grover 447

Code of Hammurabi 47–49

Cold Harbor, battle of 378

Cold war 252, 393

Collective farms 80, 222

Columbus, Christopher 242, 430, 471

*Common Sense* 435

Commonwealth of Independent States 224

Communism 14–17, 57, 58, 79–81, 196, 223, 224, 254, 274, 369, 380, 393, 394

Communist League 277

*Communist Manifesto* 277

Communist Party 221–224, 256, 258, 259

Compiègne, battle of 250

Comyn, John 301

Confederate States of America 377, 378, 407, 408, 412–414

Confederation of the Rhine 286

*Confessions* 297, 298

Confucianism 21, 23

**Confucius 21–23,** 76

Conquistadors 189, 191, 430, 433

**Constantine I** 61, 128, **197–200,** 225

Constantine VI 62, 63

Constantinople 62, 63, 101, 102, 128–130, 199, 225

Constitution of the United States 374, 420, 421, 490

Constitutional Convention 374, 490

Continental System 286

Cornwallis, Charles 489

Corsica 282, 283

Cortés, Hernán 191, 192, 430, 432, 433

**Crazy Horse 357–360,** 457

Crimean War 312

*The Crisis* (NAACP) 368

*The Crisis* (Paine) 435

Croesus 25

Crook, George 359

Crusades 101, 202, 203, 214, 215

Cuban missile crisis 394

Cuban Revolution 380–382

Cuban Revolutionary party 424
Cultural Revolution 81
Custer, George Armstrong 359,
   455, 457
**Cyrus II, the Great 24–26,** 138

**D**

Darius III 159, 160
Darnley, Henry Stewart 279,
   280
*Das Kapital* 277
Daughters of Temperance 339
**David, King 27–30,** 65
Davis, Jefferson 407, 408, 412
Declaration of Independence
   373, 384, 386, 387, 405
Deir el–Bahri, temple at 56
Deism 436
Demetrius 106
Democratic Party 392, 411, 443,
   446, 448, 449
Democratic Republicans 386,
   490
**Der Judenstaat** 11
Diadochi 105, 106
Díaz, Porfirio 496, 497
Dienbienphu, battle of 59
Diet of Worms 190, 266
Din–i–Ilahi 6
Diocletian 197–200
Directory 283, 284
Disraeli, Benjamin 313
*Domesday Book* 317
Domingue, Saint 471–473
Dominican Republic 471
Dos Ríos, battle of 425
Douglas, Stephen A. 410
**Douglass, Frederick 361–365,**
   477
Drake, Francis 205, 207
Dred Scott Case 477
**Du Bois, W. E. B. 366–369,**
   486
Dumont, John 476

**E**

East African Community 100
Eck, Johann 266
Edict of Milan 62, 199
Edict of Nantes 262
Edward I 301, 302
Edward II 302
Eightfold Path 119
Eisenhower, Dwight D. 445
Elam 8, 9
**Eleanor of Aquitaine 201–204**
**Elizabeth I 205–208,** 279, 280,
   281
Emancipation Proclamation 413
Engels, Friedrich 276, 277
Enlightenment 181, 182, 217,
   343, 385, 436
Esar–Haddon 7, 8
Estates–General 283

**F**

*Facing Mount Kenya* 69
Fallen Timbers, battle of 468
Farouk 90
Fatehpur Sikri 6
Faud I 90
Federalists 386, 490
**Ferdinand II** 189, **239–243**
Fetterman massacre 358
Feudalism 275, 314, 316
Fifteenth Amendment (U.S.
   Constitution) 340, 364
First Punic War 50
First Silesian War 218
Five Dynasties and Ten King-
   doms 136
Five Pillars of Islam 87
Ford's Theater 414
Fort Donelson 377
Fort Duquesne 488
Fort Laramie Treaty 359, 457
Fort Necessity 488
Fort Phil Kearney 358
Fort Sumter 412
Four Noble Truths 119

Fourteenth Amendment (U.S. Constitution) 340, 364
Francis I 190
**Francis of Assisi 209–211**
Franciscan Order 211
**Franklin, Benjamin 370–374,** 386, 435
Franks 184–186, 188
**Frederick I (Barbarossa) 213–215,** 233
**Frederick II, the Great 216–220**
Fredericksburg, battle of 408
French and Indian War 373, 488
French Revolution 10, 283, 435, 436, 452, 453, 471, 472
French West Africa 114
Fronde 261
Fugitive Slave Law 477, 481
Fujiwara family 31–33
Fujiwara Kaneie 32, 33
**Fujiwara Michinaga 31–33**
Fujiwara period 32

**G**

**Gandhi, Mohandas 34–38,** 94, 96, 397
Garrison, William Lloyd 363, 364
Gathas 139
**Genghis Khan 4, 39–42,** 290
Gestapo 237
Gettysburg, battle of 408
Ghazis 102
Ghost Dance 458
Glasnost 223
Golden Horde 291, 292
Gómez, Máximo 425
**Gorbachev, Mikhail 221–224**
Granada 239, 242, 243
Grand Alliance 263
**Grant, Ulysses S. 375-379,** 408, 413, 414
Great Awakening 402
Greater Colombia 342, 344, 345

Great Depression 391, 416, 442, 445, 447, 448
Great Leap Forward 81
Great Wall of China 42, 109
Greenville Treaty 468
**Gregory I, the Great 162, 185, 225–228**
Guajardo, Jesús 499
Guerrilla Warfare 382
**Guevara, Ernesto "Ché" 380–383**
**Gustavus Adolphus 229–232**

**H**

Habsburg 192, 216–218, 234, 304–306
Hagia Sophia 130
**Haile Selassie I 43–46**
Haiti 471, 472
Hamilcar Barca 50, 51
Hamilton, Alexander 386, 490
**Hammurabi 47–49**
Hampton Institute 484
**Hannibal 50–53**
Hanoi 58, 59
Hanseatic League 272
Harding, Warren G. 448
Harpers Ferry 364, 406, 481
Harrison, William Henry 469, 470
Hasdrubal 52
Hastings, battle of 314
**Hatshepsut 54–56,** 61
Hattushilis 113
Hegel, Georg Wilhelm Friedrich 275
Hegira 86
Heian period 31–33
Helena, Saint 288
Hellenism 18, 104, 105
Hellenistic civilization 104, 105
Henry II 202, 203
Henry VIII 190, 191, 205, 206, 279, 280
Herodotus 24, 25

Herzl, Theodor  11
Hinduism  5, 6, 35, 96
Hispaniola  471–473
Historical materialism  276, 277
*History of Plymouth Plantation* 348
*History of Woman Suffrage*  340, 465
**Hitler, Adolf**  12, **233–238**, 450, 451
Hittites  112, 113
**Ho Chi Minh  57–60**
Ho Chi Minh City  60
Hohenzollern  216, 220
Holocaust  12
Holy Roman Empire  190, 213, 214, 231, 233, 282, 286, 294, 295, 308
Hoover, Herbert  449
House of Commons  194–196
Howard, Oliver Otis  354
Huerta, Victoriano  498
Huguenots  262
Huitzilopochtli  431, 432
Hull House  335–337
Humanism  206
Humayun  4–6
Hundred Days battle  288
Hundred Years War  249
Hunkpapa Sioux  359, 455–457
Huns  165–167, 294
Hussein, Saddam  74

I

Iconoclasm  62
"I Have a Dream" speech  399
Imperialism  34, 57, 313
Inca  189, 192
India Act of 1935  37
Indian National Congress  36, 37, 94, 96
Indochina  57–59
Indulgences  265, 266
Industrial Revolution  57, 275, 335

Instruction  182
Iran hostage crisis  71, 73
Iran–Iraq War  74
**Irene of Athens  61–63**
**Isabella I**  189, **239–243**
Isfahan  1, 3
Istanbul  122, 124
Italian Wars  190
**Ivan IV, the Terrible  244–247**

J

Jackson, Thomas J. "Stonewall" 407, 408
Jacobins  283
Jahangir  6
Jamestown  459–461
Jamukha  40, 41
**Jefferson, Thomas**  373, **384-387**, 490
Jen  23
**Jesus of Nazareth  64–67**, 85, 117, 129, 140, 214, 402
Jim Crow laws  366, 485
**Joan of Arc  248–251**
**John XXIII  252–255**
Johnson, Lyndon  395
Johnston, Joseph E.  407
**Juana Inés de la Cruz  388–390**
Judas Iscariot  67
Justin I  129
**Justinian I  128–130**

K

Kaaba  86, 87
Kadesh, battle of  112, 113
Kai Feng  136, 137
Kalmar Union  273
Kampaku  32, 33
Kansas–Nebraska Act  410
Karnak  55, 112
**Kennedy, John F.  391–395**, 417, 421
Kenyan African National Union 70
Kenyan African Union  69

*Mein Kampf* 235, 237
Melbourne, William 311
Mendive, Rafael María de 422, 423
Menelik II 43
Mensheviks 257
Mesopotamia 47, 48
Metacomet 495
Metaurus River, battle of 52
Mexican Revolution 496–499
Mexican War 376, 378, 406
Middle Ages 1, 185, 201, 203, 214, 264, 316
Miles, Nelson 355, 359
Miranda, Francisco de 343
Missionaries of Charity 125–127
Missouri Compromise 410
**Moctezuma II** 192, **430–432**
Mohács, battle of 122
Mongols 4, 39, 40, 42, 101, 102, 289–292
Monophysitism 129, 130
Montgomery bus boycott 396, 397
Montgomery Improvement Association 397
Monts, Pierre du Gua de 351, 352
Moors 242
**Moses** 64, **82–85**
Mott, Lucretia 464
Mount Vernon 488, 491
Mughal Empire 4–6
**Muhammad** 12, **85–88**, 417
Muhammad Reza Shah Pahlevi 71–73
Muhammad, Elijah 416, 417
Muslim League 37
Muslim Mosque, Inc. 417
Mussolini, Benito 43, 45

**N**

NAACP (see National Association for the Advancement of Colored People)

Nabonidus 25
Naguib, Muhammad 91
**Napoleon I Bonaparte 282–288,** 342, 453, 473
Narragansett 494
*Narrative of Sojourner Truth* 475, 477
**Nasser, Gamal Abdal 89–92**
National American Woman Suffrage Association 340, 465
National Assembly 115, 283, 472
National Association for the Advancement of Colored People 367, 369, 419, 420, 421
National Convention 283, 436
National Federation of Settlements and Neighborhood Centers 337
National Industrial Recovery Act 450
National Negro Business League 485
National Woman Suffrage Association 340, 465
National Youth Administration 445
Natural rights 464, 465
Nazis 12, 195, 235, 236, 253, 450
Nebuchadnezzar 26
Necho 8
*Négritude* 115
**Nehru, Jawaharlal 93-96**
Nelson, Horatio 285
**Nevsky, Alexander 289–292**
New Deal 442, 445, 447, 449, 450
New Economic Policy 259
New France 350, 351
New Granada 342
Newport, Christopher 460, 461
New Spain 342, 388
Nez Percé 353–356
Niagara Movement 367
Nicaea, Second Council of 62

Seljuk Empire 101, 102
Seneca Falls Declaration of Sentiments 464
**Senghor, Léopold Sédar 114–116**
Separatists 347, 426, 493
Serfdom 257
Sessho 32, 33
Seti I 111, 112
Seven Days' battles 407
Seven Years' War 219
Shakers 401–404
Shamash–shum–ukin 8
Shanti Nagar 127
Shawnee 467–469
Shawnee Prophet 469
Sherman, William Tecumseh 414
Shiites 71, 72
Shiloh, battle of 377
**Siddhartha 117–120**
Silesia 218–220
Sinai, Mount 84
Sioux 358, 359, 455–458
**Sitting Bull 359, 455–458**
Six–Day War 92
Slavery 113, 340, 364, 376, 386, 406, 407, 410, 412–414, 465, 471–473, 475, 477, 479, 480
**Smith, John 459–462**
Social Security Act 450
Socialism 257–259, 276
Society of Free Officers 90
Solomon 30
Song (Sung) dynasty 135–137
*The Souls of Black Folk* 367
South African War 194, 313
Southern Christian Leadership Conference 398
Soviets 258
Spanish Inquisition 239, 242
Spanish Succession, War of the 263
Spotsylvania, battle of 378
Squanto 347, 348
Stalin, Joseph 196, 222, 451

Stamp Act 373, 489
Stanton, Edwin M. 414
**Stanton, Elizabeth Cady** 339, 340, **463–466**
**Stephen I 307–309**
Stoicism 269, 270
Stormtroopers 235
Strong Hearts 456
Suez Canal 91
**Suleiman 121–124**
Sun Dance 457
Sun Yat-sen 15, 79
Supreme Court, United States 397, 398, 419, 421, 477, 485
Supreme Soviet 222
Susa 9

**T**

Taharqa 8
*Tale of Genji* 33
Tanganyika 97, 98
Tanganyika African National Union 98
Tanzania, United Republic of 97–100
Tao Te Ching 75–77
Taoism 75, 76
Tartars 40, 245–247
Taylor, Zachary 376
**Tecumseh 467–469**
Temperance Movement 339
Temple of Amon–Ra 55, 56, 112
Ten Commandments 84
Ten Years' War 423
Tenochtitlán 191, 430–433
**Teresa, Mother 125–127**
Thames, battle of the 470
Thanksgiving 348
Thebes 54–56, 113
**Theodora 128–130**
Third Estate 283
Third Reich 233, 235
Thirteenth Amendment (U.S. Consitution) 414

Thirty Years' War 231, 232
Thutmose II 54, 55
Thutmose III 55
Ticino River, battle of 51
Tilly, Johannes 231
Tippecanoe, battle of 469
Toghrul 40, 41
**Toussaint L'Ouverture
472–474**
Toynbee Hall 336
Trafalgar, battle of 285
Treaty of Breslau 218
Treaty of Brest–Litovsk 259
Treaty of Dresden 219
Treaty of Northampton 302
Treaty of Paris 374, 490
Treaty of Ryswick 471
Treaty of Saint–Germain–en–
Laye 352
Treaty of Troyes 249
Treaty of Utrecht 263
Treaty of Verdun 188, 293
Treaty of Versailles 234, 237
Treaty of Zanjón 423
Trebbia River, battle of 51
Trotsky, Leon 259
Truman, Harry S. 445
**Truth, Sojourner 475–478**
**Tubman, Harriet 479–482**
Turner, Nat 480
Tuskegee Institute 483–486
Tuskegee Negro Conference
485
*Twenty Years at Hull–House*
337

**U**

Underground Railroad 479–481
Union of Soviet Socialist
Republics 221–224, 256,
259, 369, 382
United Arab Republic 91
United Nations 12, 17, 74, 91,
97, 98, 445, 451

*United States* v. *Susan B. Anthony*
340
Universal Declaration of Human
Rights 445
*Up From Slavery* 485
Uzbeks 1, 2

**V**

Valley Forge 489
Versailles 261
Versos sencillos 424
Vicksburg, siege of 378
**Victoria** 34, **310–313**
Vienna, siege of 122
Viet Cong 59
Viet Minh 58
Vietnam War 59, 394, 399
Vikings 162–164, 176, 271,
289, 314
Villa, Pancho 498
Virginia Company of London
347, 460, 461
Vishtaspa 139, 140
Voting Rights Act of 1965 399

**W**

Wallenstein, Albrecht von 231
Wampanoag 348, 494, 495
War of 1812 378, 469
Warren Commission 395
Warren, Earl 395
**Washington, Booker T.** 367,
**483–486**
**Washington, George** 378, 386,
405, 435, **487–491**
Waterloo, battle of 288
Wayne, Anthony 468
Wellington, Arthur 288
West African Economic Com-
munity 116
*What Is to Be Done?* 257
Whig party 410
Whiskey Rebellion 490
Wilderness, battle of the 378